W9-ARB-518

NCNF
24.95

WITHDRAWN

TAR HEEL TRAVELER
EATS

TAR HEEL TRAVELER EATS

EATS

FOOD JOURNEYS ACROSS NORTH CAROLINA

SCOTT MASON

Globe Pequot

Guilford, Connecticut
Helena, Montana

An Imprint of Rowman & Littlefield

CALDWELL COUNTY PUBLIC LIBRARY
120 Hospital Avenue
Lenoir, North Carolina 28645

Globe Pequot is an imprint of Rowman & Littlefield

Distributed by NATIONAL BOOK NETWORK

Copyright © 2014 Scott Mason

All photos by WRAL-TV/Capitol Broadcasting Company, Inc. Copyrighted material used with permission from WRAL-TV/Capitol Broadcasting Company, Inc. All rights reserved.

All rights reserved. No part of this book may be reproduced in any form or by any electronic or mechanical means, including information storage and retrieval systems, without written permission from the publisher, except by a reviewer who may quote passages in a review.

WRAL® is a registered trademark.

British Library Cataloguing-in-Publication Information available

Library of Congress Cataloging-in-Publication Data available

ISBN 978-1-4930-0638-0

∞™ The paper used in this publication meets the minimum requirements of American National Standard for Information Sciences—Permanence of Paper for Printed Library Materials, ANSI/NISO Z39.48-1992.

CONTENTS

She brings me coffee out of a glass pot with a black handle—she knows I like the first cup high-test. The pot's mostly full, and she wobbles it over my mug, a thick heavy mug that's a half shade off from white and chipped on the rim. My ears perk at the splash, like water smacking the bottom of a bone-dry well, and I can hardly wait to swallow that first gulp.

Her aim is slightly off and a couple of drips streak down the side. "Sorry, honey," she says and pulls a balled-up rag from her apron and flaps it open.

"No problem," I say. "I got it," and I fumble with the metal napkin dispenser at my booth. The napkins are thin as tissue paper, and I shred one trying to yank it out.

"What can I get you, shug?" she says and sets the coffeepot down. For a second I wonder about the Formica, but then what's another scorch mark? She slips a pen from her ear and pulls a pad from somewhere else deep in her apron.

"Two scrambled, grits, and toast."

"No meat?" she says and smiles. She's fiftyish, tall, and thin with a makeup-free face and blondish hair pushed under a baseball hat. Her voice drips with a southern drawl. "Honey, we got some real good country sausage today. Bacon, too."

"Sure, throw in some bacon," I say, stealing a look around while she scribbles.

The cook behind the counter swirls a pan with one hand, chops his spatula on the grill with the other, and leans over a pile of sizzling hash browns so the waitresses can scoot by. It's a typical one-butt kitchen, barely enough room for the lady ringing the register. The cash box is the old-fashioned kind, gray with hard-to-push buttons and heavy enough to double as a ship's anchor. Somebody's taped a note to the front: WE DO NOT ACCEPT DEBIT CARDS. The lady jabs and the drawer claps open, and she slips in a ten and pulls out some ones. But I also notice loose bills and change scattered about and figure that must be the I'll-get-to-it-later money. Trusting folks, for sure.

The place is pretty full today, a middle-aged-and-up crowd, and I wonder at the lonely high chairs stuffed in the corner alongside empty boxes. A neon-yellow mini sawhorse warns CAUTION: WET FLOOR, but it's propped on one leg against the jukebox.

People are seated at the counter and lounging in booths. I watch a big man with a crew cut mash together fried eggs and tomatoes and think maybe I should have ordered mine fried. Silverware scrapes, dishes clatter, and the place murmurs with twenty conversations at the same time.

I admire Dale Earnhardt Sr.'s bushy mustache. He poses from a poster next to signs that shout COUNTRY STYLE STEAK SANDWICH! and CHEESY OMELETS! Tacked nearby is a fake dollar bill three times the size of a regular one, but instead of George Washington's picture, Ronald Reagan grins and wears a cowboy hat. He probably wouldn't be so happy about Old Glory stretched on the opposite wall. The flag looks like it's been to battle and back. The white stripes aren't what they were, but to me red, yellow, and blue seem patriotic nonetheless.

"I'll bring you more coffee in a minute, sweetie," my smiley southern gal says and turns away. I like that. I've only managed one sip and she's already thinking about the refill.

I pull my laptop from my backpack, which would have felt awkward a few years ago—diners are pad-and-pencil kinds of places. But times have changed. A NO SMOKING sign dangles from a chain clamped to a ceiling tile. I've never been one for cigarettes anyway, and I'm glad the staff traded hairnets for ball caps.

And yet times haven't changed. The plastic menus are still sticky, wedged between bottles crammed together in a metal rack at my table: Texas Pete, A.1. Steak Sauce, Heinz 57. I take odd comfort in the big glass sugar dispenser and glass salt and pepper shakers, and I laugh at the thought of my germophobe friend who wipes everything down in a hotel room, especially the television remote. No napkin would be big enough for him in a place like this.

The coffee's good, and even the chipped rim feels right. I think I could sit here all day and sip and eat and tap at my computer. I want to write about places like this, this very place right here, right now, and so many others and why they're important. They're important to me, part of who I am.

My wife and kids tell me I'm old-fashioned, and they're right—or at least as old-fashioned as you can be in twenty-first-century Internet America. I occasionally zip through fast-food joints and opt for the nearest highway, but I prefer the slow lane. I like sitting a spell in a cozy booth at an old-timey place and wrapping myself in the homey atmosphere, full of warmth and friendliness and good conversation from everyday folks. They're people without pretensions but often with faded overalls, and I admire them because they're honest and real. But it's more than that. These people and places, I think, are part of a community's fabric—and broader still, part of North Carolina's fabric, the deepest part that holds everything together.

They draw me because I'm one from the old school, too, who happens to be a reporter. Just the facts, no frills, tell it like it is, plain and simple. But I'm also a reporter who specializes in features, and I like a touch of spice with my writing, and when I write about places like this I realize each one has its own distinct flavor.

I follow one swig with another and ponder my next sentence. The screen stares back, but I'm ready. The atmosphere is right, and the words will come. And so will the waitress. I see her now slipping past the counter, coming around again with the pot just like she said. That didn't take long. She even remembered to bring the orange-handled one this time—decaf—and I smile. She does, too.

"Eggs coming," she says as she pours. Her aim is perfect. "Sit long as you like. Glad to have you, hon."

"Thank you," I tell her and watch her go, and after a moment I lift the heavy mug and, what the heck, toast the laptop screen. *Aah, yes,* I think, here goes—my book: *Tar Heel Traveler Eats.*

I begin to type.

I was born in Raleigh but my family moved when I was two, and so I grew up on the coast of Massachusetts, eating lobster and clam chowder. And fish roe and grits. That's because Mom was raised in Virginia. We spent Christmas holidays at my grandmother's house in Richmond and ate black-eyed peas and stewed tomatoes on New Year's Day.

Southerners are proud of their food: biscuits and fried chicken, barbecue and collard greens. They're proud of where they eat their food: the little place with the faded awning and the worn spot on the floor by the cash register, or the grill with daily specials scrawled on a ripped piece of cardboard propped in the window.

Northerners are the same way. The first time I went to Pennsylvania I couldn't believe how many diners there were. In Massachusetts, Dunkin' Donuts is everywhere. Even at a chain, a wobbly stool and Styrofoam cup of coffee are a cozy comfort. It's true. There's a Dunkin' Donuts by the railroad tracks in Gloucester where I spent my summers, and I pop in every July when I go back. The place is usually packed with whiskered fishermen yapping to the ladies behind the counter. "Yo, Gloria. I'll take a coifee ova heeya, daarlin'." The ladies smile and yap right back, and I sit at a little table with my own "coifee" and admire the Yankee hubbub of the place. Like the jelly donut in my hand, there's a warm sweetness at its center once you get past the outer edges.

I had a kind of get-away-to-a-hole-in-the-wall-diner mind-set even as a kid. I remember Dad talking about Maxie's, which was someplace near his office in downtown New Bedford.

"What'd you do for lunch today?" Mom would ask at dinner.

"Had a salad at Maxie's." She'd throw him a hard stare, knowing he'd probably had a cheeseburger, too.

Whenever I pictured Maxie's I saw a long row of men at a counter with their shirtsleeves rolled up, slurping coffee and licking cheeseburger juice off their fingers. I wished I could go.

Years later Dad did take me, and it was exactly how I imagined. But I was still a teenager then and felt terribly self-conscious with all those guffawing grown men, and Maxie's' luster faded for me after that. That was Dad's place. One day I'd have to find my own.

I was the kind of kid who always knew what he wanted to do. I wrote lots of short stories and poems, and when I shot hockey pucks by myself in the driveway or pitched tennis balls against the garage, I'd pretend I was a play-by-play announcer calling the action.

After college I immediately plunged into television news, climbing markets over the years, landing reporter jobs at stations in Chattanooga, Winston-Salem, and Dayton. I didn't actually work in Dayton but in a blue-collar town forty minutes east. I was the Springfield bureau chief. It was 1988, and I was twenty-seven years old and single.

I often drove by a breakfast-and-lunch joint in Springfield with a warped metal sign out front: THE SPRINGFIELD RESTAURANT. It was a plain brick building; the bricks were beige and the windows tinted. In fact, the windows were black, no way to see in—maybe to hide the restaurant rating. I hadn't yet found a good local dive, so one Saturday morning I took a chance, rolled into the lot, and crept inside.

A dark room blinded me. When my eyes adjusted I noticed booths along the walls but no tables in the center, just a wide empty space. Odd, I thought, but maybe the place didn't need more tables. Maybe there weren't enough customers.

I quickly slipped into the nearest booth and flopped open my newspaper so I'd have something to do while waiting for a waitress. *Is there a waitress?*

There was. She was a petite woman pushing eighty who shuffled across the divide with a coffeepot and mug. "Thank you," I said.

"Ready to order?" I was, and she scribbled *two scrambled* in a little pad and started back across the room. It was a quick-and-easy transaction: no fuss, no chatter, no smile, but efficient. I was beginning to feel more comfortable— maybe because most of the booths were empty.

From then on I was a Springfield Restaurant regular. A year after jotting my orders, the waitress began to offer a trace of a smile. I liked her. She let me read and write and stare out the tinted window and watch half of Saturday drift by, and she'd shuffle across the room with the coffeepot when I was on my last gulp. Beats me how she knew. She just did.

I think of the happy moments in my life, the big ones: my wedding and the births of my three kids. But I cherish the small ones, too. I am so very happy in a booth with bacon, eggs, grits, and coffee, and a good book, or a good idea for a book that I peck on a laptop—or jot on a napkin when the battery drains. It's how I wrote the book you're reading. I wrote it at breakfast dives all over Raleigh.

By chance or fate I landed back where I was born. WRAL-TV hired me in 1997, and I spent the next ten years in Raleigh producing documentaries and covering general news, often sneaking away to Waffle House to write my scripts. I've probably written a hundred stories at Waffle House and never once eaten a waffle. I'm an egg man all the way.

I'm a feature man, too. If there was a county fair that needed news coverage or hot-air balloon festival or Guinness World Records breaker, the TV stations I worked for always seemed to pick me for the assignment.

WRAL did the same, to the point that most days the news director was doling out murders, fires, and car wrecks to other reporters, while sending me to interview the man with the pet alligator named Elmo two hours down the road—even telling me, "Be careful."

In 2007 WRAL finally made me its full-time feature guy, the Tar Heel Traveler, which to me is the best job in television. A photographer and I roam North Carolina, telling stories about memorable people and out-of-the-way places. The stories are about two-and-a-half minutes long and air on the news Monday through Thursday nights. They attract a large and loyal audience. People tell me they love the *Tar Heel Traveler,* especially the stories about mom-and-pop places dishing up hot dogs, hamburgers, barbecue, biscuits, donuts, and ice cream.

I tell people North Carolina is the perfect state for the work I do. There are so many great features out there, a never-ending supply, and every day viewers e-mail me even more ideas. Of course, that means I have to continually write all those stories. The work never ends. And so I slink away to a breakfast-served-anytime kind of place and slip into a booth with cracked vinyl and a cup of coffee, lots of coffee. I do my best work holed up in an old-timey restaurant, which is another reason why North Carolina is the perfect place. There's a never-ending supply of those, too.

As the Tar Heel Traveler I set out to explore as many diners as I could, or as many as the news director would allow, and what a full journey it turned out to be, loaded with good food and good people.

It's just that whenever I'd package one of these restaurant stories and watch my work unfold on air, my stomach would growl, and not just from hunger. A feeling gnawed at me that there might be something more to the stories, another layer I'd only tasted on the tip of my tongue. The more restaurant stories I covered for WRAL, the more I grew aware of tapping into something else, something important, some special ingredient inherent in the landscape of diners that dot the back roads and main streets of North Carolina and which imbues North Carolina with flavor.

The pages that follow—and I hope I haven't dribbled coffee stains on any of them—are stories about the nothin'-fancy kind of places that are close to people's hearts—maybe hard on their hearts, too; some folks still cook with lard.

The irony, I think, is that "My Little Hot Dog Book," as I sometimes call it, might just have a little more meat to it—and, by the way, it includes more than just hot dogs. As I recaptured my time sitting at counters and snuggling in booths with mustard on my cheeks or powdered sugar on my nose, poignancy crept into my thoughts, which I sprinkled between the lines without at first realizing it. *My Little Hot Dog Book tugging at heartstrings?* I mused. *Really?*

What I do know is that I love these mom-and-pop places and long to revisit them for fear they may fade away. I'm glad I told their stories on TV and maybe in some way helped preserve them—after all, video lives on in reruns.

Tar Heel Traveler Eats is an attempt to preserve these places on paper this time and add a topping that might not have been so obvious when they appeared on TV. The chapters ahead are not just about restaurants but also about culture, tradition, and heritage. At least, that's my take on My Little Hot Dog Book.

So please, grab yourself another coffee, settle in, and turn the page, and don't mind me if I'm right there with you. I can't get enough of these little places. They're what red clay is to North Carolina: a dusty but distinctive part of the foundation. And may they remain steadfast and secure.

They are North Carolina classics, and I sure hope you enjoy them as much as I do.

BILL'S HOT DOGS

IT WAS A LITTLE PLACE ALONG A SIDE STREET IN WASHINGTON, North Carolina, with a washed-out sign that read BILL'S HOT DOGS. Bill's didn't even have any tables or chairs, just a worn black-and-white checkerboard floor, scuffed and faded from the muddy boots, tasseled loafers, high heels, and high tops that tramped across it. People of all walks stood and ate, and more kept coming in, often slamming the screen door behind them. Bill's brought everybody together.

Must be some good hot dogs, I thought.

"Best there is," said a scruffy man in a ball cap who read my mind and raised his dog. "Cheers." Then he stuffed it in, mumbling, "Mmm, mmm," the whole way.

"The chili is out of this world," said a woman who might have come from the beauty parlor. Her glossy gray hair glowed with a tint of blue, and she wore bright red lipstick.

Bill's was one of those quick-and-easy feature stories that happened to fall along our path. My trustworthy photographer and I were on an overnight trip headed east, gathering as many stories as we could along the way. At Bill's all the video and sound was right there within those four yellowed walls.

> IF I HAD A NICKEL FOR EVERY HOT DOG THAT'S EVER BEEN EATEN HERE, I WOULDN'T HAVE TO WORK ANYMORE.

"If I had a nickel for every hot dog that's ever been eaten here, I wouldn't have to work anymore," said a man with a friendly chuckle.

"They're not good for your heart but good for your soul," said another who balanced a wobbly brown bag on his palm. I noticed the bottom of the bag growing dark with a splotchy stain.

We captured video of the hot dogs, which bobbed in a bubbling vat of water behind the counter—or it may have been a vat of grease, I'm not sure. A trio of hair-netted ladies operated an efficient assembly line, one with a spoon slathering mustard on the bun, another with prongs dropping in the dog, the spoon lady again heaping chili and onions on top, and then a third woman who wrapped the dog in waxed paper and sealed the ends. The hand off from one lady to the next took little more than five seconds.

"You oughta try one," garbled Scruffy in the ball cap. "Cheers," he blurted again, raising a second dog before he'd choked down the first.

I did want to try one. In fact, I wanted two with extra mustard. But it's hard to eat and work at the same time, so I focused instead on the yellowed walls.

Newspaper articles were nailed here and there, and I read about Bill's from reporters past. The place had been around for eighty years. *A tower of tradition*, I marked in my pad when I spotted the photo of a tall metal rack with buns stacked many feet high.

I glanced at a grouping of other black-and-white pictures and stopped and bent and pushed my eyes right up to one of the frames. *Is that . . . ?* Three dark-haired ladies appeared in the picture, two of them tall and skinny, one short and stout. They were frozen in the act of cooking, slathering, and wrapping. *Oh my gosh!* The workers behind the dusty glass were the ones working behind the Plexiglas, only now a little grayer and shorter, even the tall ones. *The same ladies!*

I could hardly believe it when the stout one let me step around the counter and clip a microphone to her. I felt we'd already interfered enough; our bulky TV camera seemed like a wrench in a well-greased machine, and we drew a lot of quizzical looks.

The lady waited for my question instead of slathering the bun. I was hoping she'd work and talk at the same time; interviews are always better when people act natural. "How're the hot dogs?" I asked.

"Fantastic," she said, and that's all she said, not a single slather. She'd faced who-knew-how-many hungry mouths over the years, but a tiny microphone was a different beast altogether. She was as frozen as she was in the photo, and I detected some antsy shuffling from the dozen folks waiting to place their orders. Thankfully, the lady at the vat dropped a dog into the empty bun, and the lady with the mic couldn't help but pitch in. She shoveled chili and onions on top, and the assembly line churned back to life. "The place has been here so long. Nothing's changed. Everything's stayed the same," she said and handed the dog to the waxed-paper lady who wrapped it, while I wrapped the interview. Those few simple sound bites were enough, and I swept in and snatched the mic without further interruption.

I think even some of the customers were impressed. They'd probably never heard the lady speak, only watched her work. A few more sidled over. "You oughta try one." But I was preoccupied with the script, which is why quick-and-easy stories are never quite quick and easy. I put pen to pad:

There are no tables and chairs at Bill's. Just a floor that's black and white and dogs red all over. Eighty-eight cents apiece, plain or all the way.

I made sure the photographer shot the checkerboard floor, the bright red dogs, the "88" posted on the wall. He even shot video of a small statue of a droopy-eyed hound dog propped on the counter. I thought a moment, then turned to my pad again:

The place may look sleepy, but oh, no. The dogs are runnin', and there's a run on dogs, and these dogs are on a roll.

All the while, the annoying screen door kept creaking open and slamming shut as people filed in and out. But then it occurred to me the door was part of Bill's charm. "Shoot the door," I told the photographer. The door charmed him, too. I

THE PLACE MAY LOOK SLEEPY, BUT OH, NO. THE DOGS ARE RUNNIN', AND THERE'S A RUN ON DOGS, AND THESE DOGS ARE ON A ROLL.

bet he shot the thing twenty times from twenty angles, while I wrestled with the words:

The screen door slams and Bill's is slammed. . . .

"Hey, you oughta try one," said Scruffy, bumping my arm and ruining my penmanship.

It is one of my great regrets that I did not eat a hot dog at Bill's that day. I probably could have eaten for free, the beauty of being a reporter on a restaurant story—the food is often on the house. Which is why I did not place my two-dog order with extra mustard. I didn't want the hard-working assembly-line ladies to feel any obligation. Oh, I salivated all right. I kept wondering what made the chili so tasty. It looked to me like the spoon lady was piling it on just about every dog. At that point I think I would've ordered a second one all the way: mustard, chili, *and* onions. But I knew I didn't have any mints on me, always a hazard when another interview waits for you down the road.

We aired the segment a couple weeks later, and my e-mail inbox practically exploded. I felt like the ladies at Bill's, facing a line of hungry hot-dog eaters that stretched out the screen door. They had orders to fill. I had messages to read:

Saw your piece on Bill's. Good story, but I got another one for you. . . .

Hey, you gotta check out the stand where I stay at. Best dogs around. . . .

You ain't lived till you had the hot dogs near me. I'm tellin' you. . . .

Bill's? That ain't nothin'. Looky here. . . .

I quickly compiled a long list of hot dog joints scattered across the state. *Do people really love hot dogs that much?* I wondered. But maybe it wasn't so much the food they craved. Maybe it was the places that meant so much to them. Many had stood for years, and the families that opened them often still operated them. Day after day, familiar faces behind hot dog counters all over North Carolina were boiling or grilling and slathering and wrapping, and feeding the good people of the Tar Heel State, all kinds of people. *Hmm*, I thought, *that's the story*. The places seemed a sort of hole-in-the-wall democracy.

Bill's set me on an unexpected journey to find the best hot dog in North Carolina. I studied the staggering list. Each place no doubt had a story all its own. But all those stories, all those calories. . . .

My stomach growled, and I licked my lips. From then on I vowed to sample a dog at each and every place.

Make that two dogs. With extra mustard!

Months later the photographer and I had to pass right through Washington, North Carolina, on our way to a story farther east. We looked at each other and I checked my watch. Not much time, but what the heck. We dashed into Bill's, this time without the camera, and the ladies didn't give us a second glance. We were just a couple of working men hungry for hot dogs. I ordered one with extra mustard. And another all the way. I didn't have a mint on me that day either. But, man, was it worth it.

HAP'S GRILL

I HADN'T SPENT MUCH TIME IN SALISBURY, AND I WAS CURIOUS. I did not ordinarily drink Cheerwine (a sweet red drink—fantastic when ice cold, sipped on a hot day), but I knew Cheerwine was made there. I did not usually grocery shop at Food Lion, but I knew Food Lion was based there. I admired Elizabeth Dole during her presidential run, and I knew Elizabeth Dole was from there.

But what really put me in the car and pointed it west toward Rowan County was a little hot dog place called Hap's Grill. A viewer had suggested Hap's, said it had been around for years, the people were friendly, the food great, a hot dog and cold bottle of Cheerwine definitely the best! I had to admit, he sure made the place sound nice and homey.

HAP'S IS NAMED FOR A MAN NAMED HAP. BUT HAP'S IS ALSO HALF OF HAPPY.

Salisbury is about two hours from Raleigh. I called Hap's Grill and the Cheerwine plant and set up both stories for the same day. First stop: Hap's. I'd arrive for the lunch crowd.

Back then I was working with Greg, who had a great camera eye and sharp computer mind. He slid behind the wheel, and I studied the address I'd googled off the Internet: Hap's Grill, 116.5 North Main Street. I pulled the sheet closer. "One sixteen—and a half? Hmm," I muttered. And so did Greg when he tried punching it into the navigation system, but the GPS was stumped. No dice. It accepted only round numbers, not half numbers. He plugged in 116 instead and shrugged. Close enough.

We rolled up to Hap's later than I wanted. We'd stopped for a biscuit and coffee on the way, a must for any long Tar Heel Traveler trip, even if hot dogs are at the other end of the road.

Hap's was a skinny shotgun of a building with a metal awning, and the line to get in spilled onto the sidewalk when we hustled up with our gear. "Excuse me, excuse me," I said and squeezed through the narrow doorway.

Two steps past the threshold and I was at the counter already. I half expected somebody to grab my collar and yank me back, growling, "No cuttin' the line, buddy-ro." The counter was all there was, not a table and chair in sight—not enough room. Had I spread my arms like an eagle I would have practically brushed the two walls, which were decked with old Cola signs and a black-and-white framed photo of kids from *The Little Rascals* TV show. I'd seen the show before and recognized the beanpole of a boy with a cowlick. Stubborn strands of his dark hair stood straight up in back.

"Eight-and-a-half feet wide," said a beefy man in line, gesturing from wall to wall and apparently recognizing me as a first-timer—maybe recognizing me as claustrophobic, too. He grinned. "But it's wide open."

He pointed at the man working the grill and told me he was the fella who owned the place. I watched the short-order cook a moment and marveled at his arms that moved like pistons. He reached for buns, rolled dogs, snatched the spatula, and flipped burgers while a woman over his shoulder called out orders. I finally called out, too. "I'm the TV guy from Raleigh," I said. "Mind if I put a little microphone on you?" The cook shrugged, but the pistons kept right on pumping. *Nothin' halfway about him*, I thought. *He's full throttle.*

The cook's name, like the photographer I was with, was Greg. He wore a white apron over his white shirt and sported a baseball hat, and he had trouble looking me in the eye—he was too busy with the grill. When I told him how impressed I was at his agility, he thanked me and winced at the same time. He said he'd been cooking at Hap's since he was fourteen, and now he was in his thirties, and his body was sore from all the years working the grill. "I don't have tennis elbow. I got burger elbow," he said. But he also told me he wouldn't trade jobs with anybody.

The lady over his shoulder fed him orders while I interjected questions in his other ear. "Seventy feet long," he said when I asked about the thin sliver of a building. "The place used to be an alley. Then in 1927 they put a roof on it, made a building out of it." He stabbed a dog and plopped it in a bun. "Squeezed it between 116 and 117. One sixteen and a half," he said and raked the grill with his spatula.

He told me Hap's was named for a man named Hap, and I pictured a wind-burned old-timer in overalls. I wanted to ask more, but the orders kept coming and the crowd started closing in, so I slipped outside and began interviewing customers at the curb.

It was a warm spring day, and people stood around eating hot dogs and drinking Cheerwine. "You can eat more standing up," chuckled a businessman with his sleeves rolled to his elbows and his tie tossed over his shoulder.

"Great food," said a lady crouched beside her daughter and dragging a napkin across the little girl's chin.

"Hot dogs!" the girl squealed.

"Hap's has been around for years and years, and there's nothing like it," said a plump man between bites. "I mean, people will take field trips from out of state to come and go to Hap's."

I had a good time talking to the folks outside. They were friendly and relaxed and enjoyed their lunch while leaning against long-legged wooden tables at the curb; no chairs, just tables propped beneath shady trees along Main Street. All those good people made me think of *The Little Rascals* photo I'd seen inside. I knew about that show because I'd interviewed a television historian once who told me it was one of the first times on TV kids just acted like kids, completely natural and unaffected. Same with the folks at Hap's, no pretentions at all. I watched one man stuff half his hot dog in his cheek and wipe his mouth with his hand.

After a while I slipped back inside to thank Chef Greg and ask if he had a picture of Hap in case we needed one when we edited the story. He pointed me to a backroom, and I wandered in and searched the walls for a farmer type with crows' feet. It was then my shoe bumped against a cardboard poster propped against a shelf. I crouched and looked, and staring back at me was a man in a slick dark suit and blow-dried hair posing for a political ad: HAP FOR CITY COUNCIL. *That's Hap?* I thought and wondered if his campaign had hit bottom along with his poster.

I learned later that Hap was the original owner but moved to Topsail Beach and after that retired to the Virginia mountains. I tried to picture Hap in the mountains, relaxing in overalls and wearing a ball cap turned sideways. *Nah.* But I did wonder if he ever thought of the landmark he'd left behind. At least he'd left it in good hands—and sore arms—to Chef Greg who bought Hap's from Hap in 1995.

Photographer Greg and I ordered some dogs to go and a couple of those cold bottles of Cheerwine. We were in a hurry to get to the Cheerwine plant, our next story. We thanked the nice people at Hap's and climbed in the car, cradling our drinks and dogs. And when we pulled away and finally sampled them, man, did they hit the spot. Not only that, but they helped power my pen. I scratched out part of the script on the way across town, oozing inspiration—and dripping mustard—onto the notepad teetering on my knee:

Hap's is named for a man named Hap. But Hap's is also half of Happy. The happy people who make a habit of Hap's delight in the dogs, appreciate the atmosphere, and yearn for yesteryear. And at Hap's they feel they're halfway home again.

DICK'S HOTDOG STAND

THIS IS NASH STREET IN WILSON. NATIONAL GEOGRAPHIC ONCE *named it one of the seven most beautiful thoroughfares in America. The perfect place for a hot dog stand!*

I patted myself on the back after delivering those catchy opening lines. It was a good-looking standup, me on camera introducing the story, strolling down the sidewalk along a pretty tree-lined street with Dick's Hotdog Stand plunked on the corner. Granted, it was more of a restaurant than a stand, and I sure hoped the photographer had framed the building over my shoulder—for a reporter there's no end to worry—but I felt we were off to a great start. Now if the rest of the story could look and sound as good . . .

Greg was with me that day, too. I grabbed the tripod, he lugged the camera, and we lumbered across the parking lot and banged through the door.

The noise is what hit me first, not just the hubbub of people talking and clatter of dishes, but the clutter of the place, too, the physical "noise." Dick's was like a family room stuffed with furniture, shelves full of knickknacks and walls covered with pictures. It had the cozy feel of home with a bunch of good friends in for a visit, laughing and eating and having a good time.

The man of the house was easy to spot, an older gentleman with a red apron and blue baseball cap, the only one in the room standing other than waitresses zigzagging between tables, rushing with plates piled with hot dogs and pitchers sloshing iced tea.

I watched the apron man sidle up to a booth, lean against it, and chat with the group huddled around the table. The table was bright yellow, and the padding was as green as a Granny Smith apple. The people smiled and laughed and perked up over what seemed like some exciting tidbit of news, all eyes on their jovial host. It made me want to squeeze in and join the conversation, but after a minute he moved to another bright booth and there was more happy banter.

He seemed to know everyone in the place and exuded a magnetic friendliness. Men shook his hand, women beamed. One lady clasped his wrist. "Aah, so good to see you," I think she said.

I felt out of place standing just inside the door with that bulky tripod, although I'm not sure anyone noticed; there was so much going on. I crossed the room, and apron man spotted me and the camera behind me. He'd been expecting us because I'd called to set up the story, but his face lit up just the same, and he gripped my hand. "Aah, so good to see you" is exactly what he said.

Lee Gliarmis turned to a table near the center of the room and pulled out a chair. "Sit down, sit down. How 'bout a hot dog?"

"Not just yet," I told him.

"You?" he said, cocking an eyebrow at Greg, whose pinched face told me he was in a near panic to grab the action while he could. He started aiming and shooting, and Lee shrugged. "Well, maybe we'll get him one later."

Lee and I took a seat. He reminded me of a kindly grandfather, his eyes brown and warm. He folded his arms, leaned toward me, and asked about my travels.

I told him we really loved coming to Wilson, so many great stories here, and Dick's would be a good one, too. "But who's Dick?" I asked.

Lee folded his leathery hands. He was olive skinned, and I was pretty sure that was part of his story. *Gliarmis*, I thought, mulling the name.

Lee began telling me the story of his father, Socrates Gliarmis, who traveled from Greece, opened his comfortable corner restaurant in 1921, and watched it grow into a beloved Wilson landmark.

"My wife is Greek," I interrupted, and his dark eyebrows shot skyward. "Yeah," I said. "Her grandfather came from Sparta. Rode a donkey down the mountain to catch the boat. Had a few dollars in his pocket when he left, that's all." I knew the details because my teenage daughter had just researched him for a school project on family history.

"Dad was a captain in the Greek army," Lee said and pointed at the wall and a blurry photo of his father standing at attention in full military regalia. "Ended up in Pennsylvania training Greek-American soldiers for WWI duty in France."

"My wife's grandfather started in Pennsylvania," I said. "He pushed a fruit cart in Philadelphia," and for some reason that tickled us both. I pictured wobbly wheels and a wide-eyed man grasping at falling oranges.

"That's how it starts," Lee said, grinning. "Dad came back from France and followed his brothers to Wilson. He had the hot dog stand downtown where the tobacco markets were."

I knew Wilson had been famous for tobacco. The local AM radio station is WGTM, which stands for World's Greatest Tobacco Market. What windmills are to Holland, tobacco barns are to Wilson; they're everywhere—though today many are lopsided and sagging.

"He sold hot dogs downtown for a while, then moved to an old grocery store here on Nash Street."

"So Dick's started in a grocery store?" I asked, taking notes.

"Sure did. And then a couple years later, he built this place, and that was the beginning."

It was also the beginning of Lee. He talked of his mom coming over from Greece and meeting his dad on a blind date. They married and had two sons. "My brother was killed in the Battle of the Bulge," Lee said, which froze my pen. "Nineteen forty-four."

Though I wasn't born until almost two decades later, I felt the enormous weight of that year, 1944, and its heavy historical significance as soon as Lee mentioned it. That's because my television travels once took me to Normandy, where I walked on Omaha Beach and witnessed aging veterans with tears in their eyes dig their fingers into the wet rocky sand and scoop handfuls into plastic bags. The men I saw had survived bloody Omaha on June 6, 1944, and helped change the world, and fifty years later they were back to collect the sand from the beach where so many of their comrades had fallen.

It was while producing that documentary about the fiftieth anniversary of D-day that I came to appreciate the sacrifice that occurred later in 1944 at the Battle of the Bulge, where nineteen thousand American soldiers died—one of them a man named Gliarmis.

Lee told me about his brother's death in a matter-of-fact manner, but something in his eyes made me turn away, and I realized it was the same look I'd seen in those veterans on Omaha Beach, crying as they scooped mushy sand into little bags. How sad I felt for them, and how proud at the same time, and I think that's the look I saw in their eyes as well.

It was the thick of lunch hour, and every table was full. The place hummed, except for *our* table. I waited a beat to break the moment of silence.

"Poppy was in the restaurant business, too," I said. "My wife's grandfather—Poppy. He moved to Virginia and worked at the Carnival Cookhouse in Richmond and then took over the whole carnival." That also tickled us both, until I told Lee about Poppy setting up one of the carnival tents. "Had the rope twirled around his hand when a gust of wind came and ripped off three of his fingers." We both winced.

"The Wilson circus grounds used to be right up the street," Lee said. "And before that the baseball park. Can you believe they won the league championship their first two seasons? One of the smallest towns in the country to have a Class B team. Between the circus and baseball, Dad sold a lot of hot dogs."

He leaned closer suddenly. "You know the Campbell Soup Company tried to buy his chili recipe? He wouldn't do it. Back in that generation you didn't give up any secrets. People didn't expect to become millionaires in those days."

He asked what became of the carnival, and I told him about Marks Shows. "Largest traveling carnival on the East Coast in the 1940s," I said. "They called it the Mile Long Pleasure Trail. You know the Flying Wallendas?" His eyebrows shot up again. "They were part of the act, walked the high wire without a net. We even have an autographed picture of them on the wall at home."

Lee shook his head. "Amazing," he said.

Lee had his own autographed pictures, hundreds framed and hung on the walls all around the restaurant. He pointed out some of the notables: North Carolina natives Andy Griffith and Ava Gardner, Clint Eastwood, Burt Reynolds, and Jodie Foster. President Jimmy Carter was on the wall, and baseball heroes Bob Uecker and Boog Powell. There were scads of other athletes, too, both local and national.

"On Saturday nights Dad would set up a boxing ring in the parking lot and hold amateur fights," Lee told me. "He'd pay the winner three dollars and the loser a dollar and a half." We both laughed.

"I planned on being a baseball coach," Lee said. "But then Dad got sick, and I came back to help out. He died in '51, and I've been here ever since."

I jotted all this down on my notepad. It was good stuff, but we hadn't recorded a single bit on camera. I started to look for Greg when I heard a *whomp!* The kitchen door had flung open, and the tripod legs came poking out, followed by Greg, his shirt collar yanked halfway off by the heavy camera strapped across his shoulder. *Man, he needs some iced tea*, I thought. But no time for that. I waved him over, and he shifted his gear, put his head down, and plowed through the dining room.

"This community has been great to my family and the business," Lee told me on camera. He said a few other good comments, although he'd actually been

better off camera. I'd done it again, tired out the interviewee before the interview. Always best to roll right away before your subject talks himself out. But, oh well. I'd enjoyed our private chat. I could always paraphrase what he'd said.

We stood and Lee clutched my elbow. "The greatest picture is the one up there." He pointed to a framed portrait of two toddlers above the counter. "My grandchildren." One of the boys was noshing on a hot dog nearly bigger than he was, but just the dog. His brother had snatched the bun.

Lee showed me to the counter, his hand on my back, and introduced me to his son, Socrates, who worked the register. "My dad has meant a lot to this community," Soc said with camera rolling, "as I'm sure my grandfather did. This is a restaurant that's been in the same family for eighty-seven years, and you don't find that very often."

We'd been in Dick's for a while, and I was antsy to interview the lunch crowd before folks slipped away. I approached two ladies in a booth, talking with their hands.

"On Sundays after church there's a mad rush from the Methodists to get up here before the Episcopalians." They cackled, and, oh, what a nice little gem of a sound bite.

I worked the microphone around the restaurant.

"You couldn't ask for a nicer place."

"Best hot dog I've ever eaten."

"I've known Mr. Lee a long time. Down to earth and friendly to everybody."

I finally felt I had the sound I needed and squeezed into a chair at a table along the wall, while Greg continued shooting. A photographer's work is never done.

I was glad for my time alone, just me and my notepad, although a blank page is never good company. How to write the story . . .

I took in the room like a fly on the wall, eavesdropped on conversations, and caught snatches of gossip and good humor. I watched the people, how animated they all were, and observed the zigzagging waitresses, balancing trays between tables, and yet their smiles never teetered. They looked happy being busy.

I took in all those pictures, too. They were mesmerizing, like staring at a collage and seeing something different every time. But they were also similar, people with arms slung around one another, everyone grinning.

I looked down at the blank page, still blank, but now a shadow cut across it. I glanced up to see Lee clutching two take-out boxes. "For you and your pretty wife." I stood, and he bundled them in my arms. They were heavy and full; the lids barely clung to the clips that held them shut, and I was afraid the stack might wobble off my arms and smack the floor.

"My wife will love them," I said. "And I will, too." He also loaded up Greg, who'd finally powered down the camera, and for the first time that day I saw him smile.

We thanked Lee and made our way outside, and it was then I noticed the large sign in the window: FOUNDED BY SOCRATES "DICK" GLIARMIS. I wondered how he'd chosen the name Dick and thought of Poppy, who'd changed his name from Eoanney to John and Mondrukas to Marks and how he couldn't speak English when he came to America. I pictured him bobbing down the mountain on an overloaded donkey, and for some reason the Flying Wallendas whirled through my head. Dick and Poppy had both stepped out on a limb without a safety net.

> I TOOK IN THE ROOM LIKE A FLY ON THE WALL, EAVESDROPPED ON CONVERSATIONS, AND CAUGHT SNATCHES OF GOSSIP AND GOOD HUMOR. I WATCHED THE PEOPLE, HOW ANIMATED THEY ALL WERE, AND OBSERVED THE ZIGZAGGING WAITRESSES, BALANCING TRAYS BETWEEN TABLES, AND YET THEIR SMILES NEVER TEETERED. THEY LOOKED HAPPY BEING BUSY.

I was having trouble keeping the container lids clamped, and the succulent smell of hot dogs and mustard wafted out. I breathed it in but caught another scent, too—the fragrant smell of springtime. Those were some mighty pretty trees. *No wonder* National Geographic *named this stretch one of the most beautiful thoroughfares in America*, I thought. *The perfect place for a hot dog stand.* I smiled at the irony but also how right it felt. It seemed the ideal place to cultivate the American dream and watch it blossom.

I turned my face to the sun and felt my heart warmed.

SHORTY'S FAMOUS HOT DOGS

I WAS SEATED IN THE BACK SEAT OF A CHEVY SUBURBAN WITH 499,995 miles on the odometer, just five measly miles before the half-million milestone.

Merrie was behind the wheel, and Merrie was merry indeed. She bubbled with giddy chatter, told me all about driving cross-country on family vacations and shuttling her kids to and from college back when they were in college, and now she was carrying her kids' kids around town; belted next to me was a child's car seat. Oh, the good times they'd had, she said, and still the car kept trucking along. In sixteen years it had never broken down, and about all she ever did was change the oil.

Merrie drove with the window halfway down, pointing out sights—the middle school in Wake Forest, for example, where her children went so many years ago. The wind caught her hair, and wispy blonde strands flew about her face, but Merrie didn't seem to care. She never even looked at the camera aimed at her in the front seat. She was as natural an interviewee as I'd ever met.

Three miles to go now, and I was as excited as she was. This was going to be a great story, but, man, the anticipation. I longed for the money shot, the odometer roll, the *five* followed by all those zeroes.

Merrie herself was an added bonus, a spectacular tour guide. I could have listened to that bubbly personality for a hundred miles, and I kept bolting upright in the backseat, forgetting the reason I was there. *Jeez, I gotta remember the odometer!*

We rolled down Main and got stuck at a light, and Merrie turned and pointed to the awning outside the passenger window. "Been to Shorty's?" she asked.

"No," I said and peered beyond my own window, trying to see inside the brick building, but I couldn't get past the glare that bounced off the storefront glass.

"What? You mean you haven't been to Shorty's?" she harrumphed, and for a second I thought she might lay on the horn. But instead she began painting a picture of the landmark hot dog joint long after the light turned green. What really caught my attention was when she mentioned something about Arnold Palmer eating there.

"Arnold Palmer?" I asked. "The golfer?"

"Oh, yeah," she said. "That's his favorite restaurant."

"Shorty's?" I ripped a sheet from my pad and scribbled myself a note.

"Oh, look. One more mile!" Merrie shrieked, and I jumped so high I nearly smashed the interior light with my head.

She never did finish the story about Arnold Palmer, but she did complete the mission. "There it is!" she squealed when 499,999 rolled into 500,000. "It's like a baby being born! There it is! It's beautiful." Her eyes went watery.

"You must love your car?" I asked.

"I do love my car," she said. "It's the best, it's really the best." She patted the steering wheel and peered down the road at the setting sun. "It's going to bring me safely home one more time."

It was months before I ran across the crumpled note I'd stuffed in the bowels of my backpack. I tilted it left and right and deciphered my slanted handwriting. *Shorty's. Arnold Palmer.* I smiled at the memory of Merrie.

She had merrily notched one mile at a time, and in a way that's what I was doing, racking up one story after another. In fact, I'd recently reached my own milestone: I'd visited my one-hundredth North Carolina county and aired my one-thousandth Tar Heel Traveler story, a feat accomplished in five-and-a-half years.

I thought of all the stories and miles, and I thought of Merrie and the miles *she'd* traveled. As far as I knew she was still driving her Chevy Suburban. I pictured her with the window down, humming a tune, hair swirling, odometer rolling. I grinned at the image. She made me want to hit the road again. And so did my crumply note. *My* journey wasn't finished either.

Shorty's. Arnold Palmer. I tucked the paper in my shirt pocket and felt the tug of another story—and another hot dog.

I opened the door to the oldest restaurant in Wake Forest and immediately felt safe and secure when it shut behind me, sealing me inside a dark getaway, burbling with many conversations and sizzling with smells that had me craving a burger with extra cheese and a dog or two with extra mustard.

A long line snaked from the cash register, and I realized the routine was to order at the counter and take it to go or sit and eat. I grew impressed with the big fella ringing up customers and calling out orders. "Two all the way!" He took bills and handed back change. "Thank you, bub." And then on to the next one. "Burger, lettuce, tomato, ketchup, fry." The big fella did it all so rhythmically, not the least bit flustered by the stack of faces in front of him. "How you doin' today? What can I get you?" I had the feeling he knew most everybody. "Thank you, bub." He called everybody "bub."

The cook alongside him didn't seem stressed either, even though he faced a full grill, barely enough space to fit another frank. He rolled and flipped, scooped orders onto plates, and kept his ear to the big fella. What a tandem they were; in fact, they even looked alike, and soon it all made sense. The cook was the only one who didn't go by bub. The big fella called *him* Dad.

Dad was Bill Joyner. "I'm sixty, and I started here when I was eleven years old," Bill said. He wore a red Jesse Jones baseball hat, black T-shirt, and gray whiskers and told me Shorty's started with his grandfather and an uncle named Shorty back in 1916.

"Nineteen sixteen?" I said. "Well, that's almost a hundred years."

"We been around a while," said his son, Chris, who called out another order. "Cheeseburger, chili cheese, hot dog, and a tea," he said, ringing the register and pointing his thumb at his pop. "His dad before him, and him, and now it's me. Special place. It's all special." He handed change to the man in front of him. "Thank you, bub."

An older man at the counter told me he'd been eating at Shorty's since 1942, and I stepped back and looked him up and down. He was tall and thin,

I OPENED THE DOOR TO THE OLDEST RESTAURANT IN WAKE FOREST AND IMMEDIATELY FELT SAFE AND SECURE WHEN IT SHUT BEHIND ME, SEALING ME INSIDE A DARK GETAWAY, BURBLING WITH MANY CONVERSATIONS AND SIZZLING WITH SMELLS THAT HAD ME CRAVING A BURGER WITH EXTRA CHEESE AND A DOG OR TWO WITH EXTRA MUSTARD.

especially thin for dining on Shorty's hot dogs so long. "That's over seventy years," I said.

He dug his hands in his pockets and shrugged. "I think it's a pretty good place myself."

The whole place had an air of understatement, but then most places like Shorty's do—nothing to knock you over on the outside, but inside makes your head swivel. I inventoried all the old metal signs around the room, dinged and dented ads, faded yet stamped with nostalgia. One showed a grinning kid with plump cheeks clutching a half-bitten hot dog. PLUMP, JUICY, TENDER! read the tag line, and I copied it in my pad, thinking I might write it into my story. I wrote down another line, too, a lame one that came to me and that I couldn't shake, a term I'd tussled with many times over, wrestling with myself to keep that darn cliché off the page of my hot dog stories. But shoot, it just seemed to fit: *hole-in-the-wall*.

I think of a hole-in-the-wall not so much as a flaw but more like a distinguishing characteristic, a little nook carved out of life's concrete jungle, a blip in the monotonous mainstream, a place that may have some jagged edges but is tucked away, often overlooked yet always there, safe, sheltered, never changing. You duck in, eat, talk, laugh, and just act yourself. Everybody's friendly. Everybody's "bub." I liked being called bub.

But what about Arnold?

Chris told me between register rings that the legendary golfer had graduated from Wake Forest College before the college became the university and before the school moved to Winston-Salem and that Arnold still stopped in when he was in town. "Had his eightieth birthday party here in 2003, I think it was," Chris said and showed me pictures of Palmer posing out front under the awning.

He wasn't the only celebrity from Wake Forest College to become a Shorty's regular. Carroll O'Connor enrolled in 1941, and Bill at the grill told me the future small-screen star used to come in and shoot pool. O'Connor became a TV icon for his role as Archie Bunker in the 1970s comedy sitcom *All in the Family* and later played a small-town Mississippi police chief in the drama series *In the Heat of the Night*. "And he claimed he learned his southern drawl here at Shorty's when he was shooting nine ball," Bill said.

Shorty's in fact started as a pool room, and people still racked 'em up in back. I peeked through a doorway and saw several handsome tables with fine green felt beneath a dim light.

The place was all about tradition. And all about hot dogs. "I don't know, it just tastes like a good old hot dog's supposed to taste," a lady said, pinching her lunch between her fingers. "They're grilled rather than boiled, and I like the soft buns." She poked and prodded and modeled it for the camera, and I felt like snatching it from her hand and finishing what she'd started. But the lady finally took a bite, and we grabbed the shot we'd been waiting for.

Before we left Shorty's I treated myself to my own hot dog and stumbled into a conversation. A big bearded man with a rosy Santa Claus face gripped my hand and introduced himself as Bubba—Bub for short—and he was so friendly that, Jiminy Christmas, I felt like I'd known him for years. Bubba spun me a story about secret Civil War gold. He talked of clues carved on trees and maps buried in underground vaults pointing to the hidden treasure. He was dead serious and said he and a buddy had spent years digging through dusty files. He drummed on and I warmed to the thrill in his voice and wrote down his number, thinking I might call him later and set up a story. But I didn't bother to write down his name. I knew I'd remember it. Bub.

Secret gold? Underground vaults? The news hounds back at the station would be rolling their eyes. But I liked Bubba, and it felt right meeting him at the end of my Shorty's visit, sort of like completing the circle—or circling the hole.

It was Merrie's story that had led me to this beloved hole-in-the-wall, and her words came back to me now: *My mama believed you could do anything as long as you were willing to work hard. I've taken good care of my car, and maybe that's a good lesson for all of us, to appreciate what we have.*

My eyes drifted over Bubba's shoulder, and I took in the husbands and wives, grandfolks and grandkids, men in work boots seated at the counter sipping iced tea, the thin man who told me he'd been coming to Shorty's for seventy years. *That's to the moon and back!* Merrie had exclaimed when the odometer hit 500,000. *This is how I feel about my car: It's like family.*

One story leads to another, leads to another: Merrie to Shorty's, Shorty's to Bubba, and Bubba maybe to gold! I gripped hands with Bubba and said I hoped to be in touch. "Thank you, Bub," I told him.

I turned and waved to Chris and Bill, walked out of Shorty's, and stepped from under the awning back into the bright sunlight, leaving behind a hidden treasure, safely tucked into a hole in a wall.

JIM'S OLE TIME
HOT DOGS

CHARLES KURALT USED TO TALK ABOUT THE FREEDOM OF THE road. He was a North Carolinian and CBS newsman who traveled the country telling gentle stories of people and places, a beloved reporter with a gifted voice. As a teenager I watched his Sunday morning program on television and felt like he was speaking to me. "I wanna do what he does," I used to say.

Kuralt also spoke of the romance of the road, but *he'd* wandered America in a motor home. Our Tar Heel Traveler rig is a plain Ford Taurus that rarely ventures beyond the North Carolina border. But that's okay. There are so many great stories within the state, an almost endless supply. As Kuralt himself once put it, "All you really have to do is look out the window."

I sorted through the long list of hot dog dives people had sent me, savoring the possibilities. Asheville? Boone? *Mountains might be nice this time of year*, I thought. *Or the coast.* Manteo, Nags Head. I had printed the e-mails and titled each page with the name of the town: Beaufort, Blowing Rock, Burnsville, Buxton. And then I came to the Cs: Cary, Cary, and another Cary. Each of those e-mails described the same Cary hot dog stand. One note in particular grabbed my interest:

Dear Tar Heel Traveler, You gotta meet the most hardworking, warm-hearted man there is. His name's Jim Rivers. Jim gave up a good paying sales job to sell hot dogs, and he's about the happiest man I know. He sells them at Lowe's Hardware in Cary, right outside the door, and I'm telling you his hot dogs are fantastic, best in North Carolina in my opinion. Please go visit Jim. I promise you won't be disappointed.

I was impressed by the sentiment but discouraged by the location. Cary was practically in my backyard. And at Lowe's? I tossed the Cs aside and went riffling through the Ds and Es: Dunn, Dillsboro, Elizabeth City, Elizabethtown. I licked my lips at the descriptions of good eats in faraway locales. *Plump, juicy, tender, cooked just right, and there's always a crowd. Please come visit us!*

I admired all the invitations, but that line about the most hardworking, warmhearted man kept poking at my empty stomach. I sighed and plunked down the Ds and Es and reached for the scattered Cs. And extended a hand to Jim Rivers.

I second-guessed my decision when Greg and I slipped into a parking space at Lowe's. We had to park far from the entrance; homeowners and handymen apparently shop on their lunch break and grab the closest spots. People passed us pushing shopping carts loaded with plants and plywood, and I wondered if Jim's hot dogs were the prefab variety, made weeks ago in a factory and wrapped by machine. *Kuralt wouldn't have been caught near this place*, I thought. And besides, he would've been forced to park his motor home a half mile away.

I spotted the hot dog stand tucked against the building's brick wall, to the left of the automatic double doors. A red-and-yellow umbrella tottered above a man bent over a metal box. Six or eight people clustered around, and I glimpsed a banner across the chrome that read JIM'S OLE TIME HOT DOGS!

Jim's shiny box had little compartments on top. He pulled out buns, dogs, drinks, and chips and treated the dogs with mustard, ketchup, onions, and chili. He kept the chili in a big pot. I watched him scoop a hunk and bang the spoon's neck on the rim so the excess plopped back in. The man definitely had a system, but I also wondered if he had a sore back. All that bending—I noticed an empty canvas chair ten feet behind him.

I walked up and introduced myself. Jim had small bright eyes and a round face, deeply tanned despite the umbrella. "Hey, buddy!" he exclaimed. "Make yourself at home. Get you a hot dog, something to drink?"

"No, no," I told him. "But can I hook this little microphone to you? Keep doing your thing."

I stepped back and Greg set the camera on the tripod and zoomed in from forty feet away, and the two of us began eavesdropping. The wireless mic transmitted Jim's voice, and I could clearly hear him through the camera. "Mustard, chili, onions?" It also picked up the sound of the lids: *whump* when Jim threw one open, *thunk* when he slammed it shut. *Ding, ding* when he banged the chili spoon on the pot rim. *Whoosh* when he shook open a paper bag to stuff in the dogs. "How you doin'?!" Jim greeted each customer like they were old pals.

It was beautiful is what it was, a symphony of sound, natural and unrehearsed. "Come on in the house!" Jim bellowed to a husband and wife holding hands and headed for the Lowe's entrance. *The romance of the road*, I thought. *Okay, so the road's a parking lot.* But I suddenly felt glad to be there in spite of my long list of As to Zs—even nearby Zebulon had a ring of the exotic. But Cary had Jim. "We relish your patronage!" he said, laughing and handing two dogs to a young mother.

Lunchtime was starting to slip by, and I moved in to catch some of the loyal patrons of Jim's Ole Time Hot Dogs.

"I've known Jim a lot of years, and he puts out an awfully good product," said an older gentleman who told me he visited Jim almost every day.

"The flavor, it's just so good," said a woman with a couple of *hot* hot dogs in her hand; she kept shifting them from one hand to the other. "Tell 'em to come on," she squealed. "Best hot dogs around!"

"The mayor of mustard, the sultan of slaw. I mean, no one else can compete," said a businessman in a blue blazer.

All walks of life walked up to Jim, people pushing pansies through the double doors and those lugging out lumber, the rich and not-so rich, young and old, northern and southern. It was a microcosm of America is what it was, which made me think of Kuralt again and the stories he told of ordinary people. But within those people were extraordinary stories of loyalty and hard work, commitment and compassion. I watched Jim cradle another dog and pass it gently across the counter to an elderly woman with a cane. "Oh!" the woman declared, eyes wide and mouth open. She hooked the cane to her wrist and took the dog like a little girl accepting cotton candy from her dad. "Thank you, thank you," she said, and it occurred to me this might be the happiest moment of her day. *Kuralt would have loved this*, I thought. But sadly, Kuralt was gone. He died in 1997 on the Fourth of July—a man who'd honored America in life as well as death.

ALL WALKS OF LIFE WALKED UP TO JIM, PEOPLE PUSHING PANSIES THROUGH THE DOUBLE DOORS AND THOSE LUGGING OUT LUMBER, THE RICH AND NOT-SO RICH, YOUNG AND OLD, NORTHERN AND SOUTHERN. IT WAS A MICROCOSM OF AMERICA IS WHAT IT WAS.

I finally interrupted Jim, and his customers didn't seem to mind. I think they were glad he was getting the glory he was due—though maybe not the rest his feet needed. "Folks ask me about my chair over there, and I tell them I don't get to sit in it too often," he said with a sheepish grin.

Jim told me he'd done enough sitting when he worked for a food broker peddling product lines to grocery stores in three states, burning up the road and missing his family. "I traveled for thirty years, and quite honestly that was enough. I just wanted to have something simple, but I wanted to do it the best."

Kuralt used to say, "The thrill is not reaching the destination but experiencing the journey." I mulled the old adage and thought, *Well, but I suppose it's how you look at it.* Jim had pulled off the road but embarked on a whole *new* journey—and had landed on his feet.

"What's up, my man?" he shouted to a Lowe's worker corralling shopping carts in the parking lot. The man waved.

Sometimes I think reporters can get *too* close to a story; a little perspective always helps, and so I stepped back again to take it all in. I took note of the shiny stand and brick wall, the wobbly umbrella and empty chair, and the automatic double doors. I made up my mind to script them into the story and turned to my notepad. *For Jim, the dogs have opened a door.*

I looked and listened and heard again the *whump* and *thunk* of the lids, the *ding, ding* of the spoon, and the *whoosh* of the paper bag. "Here you go, my man! Two all the way!"

My son, Scout, doesn't like hot dogs. "But why?" I ask. "I mean, they're good. Squirt some mustard on 'em, a little mayonnaise." He scrunches his nose. *Shouldn't have mentioned the mayo,* I think.

Scout was with me one Saturday when I was running errands. I had to pick up some air filters for the house. Or maybe it was lightbulbs. I slipped into the Cary Lowe's and noticed Jim had a crowd around him. *He's busy,* I thought. *I won't bother him.*

I bought filters, bulbs, and a cart full of other just-in-case house stuff. It took me almost an hour and lots of arm tugging from Scout. "I'm hungry," he said.

I pushed the cart out the door and noticed the hot dog crowd had thinned. "Hey Jim," I called, spur of the moment.

"Hey, buddy!" he said. His round face beamed. "Oh, man, I loved the story. So many people saw it. Come up to me all the time calling me Mr. Hollywood, you know." He shook with laughter. "Oh, it was just great. I can't thank you enough."

I introduced him to Scout, and Jim shook his hand and patted his head and immediately went to work. *Whump.* "How you want it, Scout?"

I was about to pipe in and say extra mustard since I figured I'd be the one eating. But Scout didn't hesitate. "Ketchup!" I narrowed my eyes at him with a look that said, *But you don't like hot dogs.*

Thunk went the lid. Scout held out his hands, and Jim set the dog in his palms. It was plump and brown with a squiggly red line across the top. Scout raised it to his mouth, Jim grinned while I held my breath, and Scout sunk in his teeth and chewed.

"*That* is the best hot dog I've ever had," he said without bothering to wipe the ketchup streak off his cheek. Jim laughed, and I sighed.

Scout still does not like hot dogs. I don't understand it. "But what about Jim's?"

"Jimmy's are different," he says. Scout calls him Jimmy like they're best buddies. In fact, sometimes Scout asks if we can go to Lowe's just so we can have one of Jimmy's hot dogs.

"Great to see you again," Jim says and beams. "How you doin', Scout? Ketchup again?"

BUD'S GRILL

I WINCE WHEN I REMEMBER THE DAYS BEFORE I BECAME THE TAR Heel Traveler. Instead of finding fun features along leisurely back roads, I covered murders, fires, and car wrecks and slapped together stories for the noon, five, and six o'clock newscasts, and it was all LIVE, LIVE, LIVE! If I had to be live on air at 6:00 p.m., I wanted to be live in Raleigh or someplace close by. That way I could be home in time for dinner.

Every morning the news managers huddled around a long table in the back conference room and doled out assignments. I tried my best to avoid the morning meeting, even though I was expected to throw a few story ideas on the table each day. But it seemed like whenever I mentioned one I was excited about, the news honchos guffawed and tossed it aside, which left me at their mercy, fretting over what god-awful story they were going to dump my way. The morning meeting was like Russian roulette, but the chamber always seemed loaded, and nine times out of ten, I took a bullet.

One day I slumped out of the room and nearly bumped into one of the photographers. "What they give you today?" he chirped. Photographers, I decided, were the smart ones. Most of them skipped the morning meeting—"Screw 'em," they'd say—even though they were supposed to show up, too.

This one looked me over, frowned, and shook his head. "Let me guess. Live shot at six in Tarboro. Tsk, tsk," he clucked and patted my shoulder. I appreciated his pity, but when he walked away, I thought I heard him laugh.

I can't remember what the honchos heaped on me that morning, but everybody in the newsroom knew Tarboro was a metaphor for no-man's-land, Siberia, hell on earth, the last place in the world you wanted to be stuck live at 6:00 p.m.

In 1997 Hurricane Floyd flooded dozens of Tarboro homes and businesses. Reporters and photographers spent so much time covering the cleanup they came to dread the moldy, musty, rank-smelling wasteland, and the image stuck in their minds like mud.

But in truth Tarboro wasn't that bad, just an eighty-minute drive east of Raleigh. And later, as the Tar Heel Traveler, I met many good people there.

I once did a story on Richard, who at seventy-three looked fit and trim in short sleeves, shorts, and sneakers. Richard walked three miles a day every day around Tarboro and kept meticulous records of his routes, dates, and distances. When I caught up with him, he'd been walking twenty years and had surpassed twenty thousand miles. He pointed to the latest entry in his ledger: 20,336— almost equal to the circumference of the earth. "I get up in the morning and away I go," he said, and I envied his vigor while checking out his shoes. *Maybe I should get my own pair of New Balance and follow in his footsteps*, I thought. *The man's an inspiration.*

Richard said three miles took him fifty-five minutes, and that's when he did his best thinking. He thought of his joys. And he thought of his wife. They'd been married forty-nine years when she died. "Best friend I ever had," he said, and his eyes fell to his ledger. He walked through life alone now, though grief was never far behind. But Richard kept to his routine. "I feel good," he said, and I admired him for both his strength and dedication. He carried on one day at a time, one step at a time, mile after mile after mile.

Another time I interviewed a ten-year-old girl who collected fossils around Tarboro. Gabrielle found them five minutes from home in a woodsy area near a creek. She dug up things like fossilized whale ribs and sea urchins that were sixty-five million years old. I'm not kidding. These were honest-to-God prehistoric remnants from dinosaur times. Something about the topography of Tarboro had preserved them.

Gabrielle wore her brown hair in bangs and looked cute in a pretty pink sweater, but she spoke like a scientific expert. She showed me her kitchen table full of fossils, which to me looked like funny-shaped rocks I would have kicked into the creek. "These are tusk shells from the Triassic period," she said. "And over here are megalodon's teeth." I opened my eyes wide and nodded, trying to show how impressed I was—and I certainly was. It's just that I had no idea what tusk and megalodon were, but I wasn't going to let a fifth grader know that. I aahed and hmmed and made a show of documenting her finds in my notepad. *But how the heck do you spell* megalodon? I wondered. (Later, I researched the word and learned that megaladon is an extinct species of shark and that the word itself is Greek for "big tooth.")

Gabrielle told me she'd received interest from museums around the world. I aahed again and congratulated her, and when she smiled I grinned at the dimples in her cheeks. I shut my notepad then and asked her what she wanted to be when she grew up. "A paleontologist," she said, which didn't surprise me. I flipped open my pad again. *Hmm, how do you spell* paleontologist?

I covered stories like that and thought, *Man, Tarboro is a hotbed of great features.* But most news people tended to see the place as a hard-luck town and sad symbol of eastern North Carolina. For God's sake, never in a million years—or sixty-five million years—did you want to be live at six in Tarboro.

But thankfully, those run-and-gun days were over for me. No more hard news or live shots. I was WRAL's full-time feature reporter now with freedom to roam almost anywhere I wanted and cover nearly any story I pleased.

So I thought I might be crazy that January day when I climbed in the car. Robert was the photographer behind the wheel. "Where to?" he said, rubbing his hands against the cold.

"Siberia," I said, and he flashed me a scrunched-up look and blew a blast of hot air on his fingers. "I mean, Tarboro."

I showed him the note somebody had written me that was sprinkled with lots of juicy description about a place called Bud's Grill. The note said *Burgers dripping with cheese!* I was hungry just from reading, and I think Robert grew famished from listening. He punched the pedal and we made it to Tarboro in seventy minutes instead of eighty.

Bud's squatted on a corner near downtown, a quaint little boxy building with a red awning. I learned when I walked in that it had been open just five years, which tempted me to walk out. A classic diner that's only five years old? A true mom-and-pop has age, tradition, character.

And yet the place was packed, the counter full. "We have people eat up here all day," said Bud, a stocky fireplug of a man with a trace of a mustache. "You look around, everybody's laughing, having a good time." He opened every morning at five thirty, and some folks ate cheeseburgers for breakfast and eggs for lunch. Bud bopped the countertop with his fist. "No need to come if you're on a diet!"

BUD BOPPED THE COUNTERTOP WITH HIS FIST. "NO NEED TO COME IF YOU'RE ON A DIET!"

The counter stretched nearly the length of the restaurant, and tables and booths lined the wall by the windows. So maybe the place wasn't old enough to be a classic, but there were definitely classics all around. My eyes fell on Chevys, Mustangs, and Cadillacs tacked, taped, and framed high and low. I studied the pictures and noted the whitewalls. "Sometimes we've had twenty, thirty old cars up here," Bud said, pointing at the parking lot. "Follow me."

We walked outside and faced the front of Bud's Grill, where a colorful mural covered the whole left side. I hadn't noticed it at first because Robert and I had approached from the other direction, but there it was, the classic diner I'd been looking for, a place where pretty girls on roller skates served burgers and shakes at your car window. An artist had captured the image in bright reds and yellows.

Bud waved his arm across the mural and told me it was the old Hollywood Drive In, a one-time local landmark that drew crew-cut kids in hot-rod roadsters and that used to sit on this very spot till it met with a bulldozer. I was impressed, and not just by the paint job. Bud could have swept the old memories under his new welcome mat but instead kept the place alive by showcasing it on *his* place. He leaned back and admired the scene, and a few of Bud's friends walked up and leaned back, too.

"That's Bud's Barracuda," somebody said, pointing to a corner. "And that yellow Buick there, that's Jim's." Bud and Jim and their friends owned classic cars themselves, and the artist had worked them into the painting.

Jim stood so close to the mural the bill of his baseball hat brushed the wall and turned lopsided on his head. He was like a wide-eyed kid with a hot fudge sundae. I asked him what he thought about seeing his Buick up there. I could tell he was nervous and didn't know what to say; he dug his hands in his pockets and shuffled his feet. "Good," he finally muttered and bobbed his head, but that was enough. I figured I'd get some mileage out of his one-word answer, head bob, and grin. His face beamed as bright as the mural in the noonday sun.

The men chatted, and I caught the same bits of conversation I'd heard inside—talk of jobs and lean times. I learned that Bud and his friends had poured their careers into textiles but the plants had closed and laid everyone off.

I began to think this was a twist I couldn't ignore but wished I could. Unemployment statistics and cold reality can slam the brakes on a warm feature. But then, Bud's Grill started *because* of the layoffs. Bud needed something to do, and his friends needed someplace to go.

"In a small way, is Bud's a beacon of hope?" I asked Charles, a Bud's regular.

"Well, it is because it's a gathering place for all those people who used to work at Dixie Yarn and Pillowtex. It *is* a beacon. It's a great place for us to come and visit."

Others shared the same feeling, even those still out of work. Money was tight, but at least they could commiserate with friends over sweet tea and a hot dog without emptying their wallets.

"We got the *best* hot dogs!" barked Shelia Mae, the short-order cook whose throaty voice sounded like my old '69 Volvo with the hole in the muffler I never

bothered to patch. But that baby was one reliable rig, and I had the feeling Sheila Mae was, too—pedal to the metal, a mile a minute, cook it up, pile it high, "Order ready!" and on to the next one. She plopped huge hamburger patties on the grill, flipped them, and gobbed them with red sauce and mozzarella cheese. "Pizza burgers," she said. "Oh, you gotta try one." She said the pizza burgers were as popular as the hot dogs.

In time I had my story, one about Bud's Grill, old cars, and lost jobs, each of them parts to what had become a fine-tuned machine at the corner. "Coming right up!" cried Sheila Mae. And to top it off there was the Hollywood Drive In, that colorful mural like a hood ornament pointing the way. And it was okay to point to the past in spite of plant closings, hurricanes, and all the other hardships Tarboro had endured. It was okay because there were so many fond memories, too. I thought of Jim, admiring his old Buick. "Good," he'd muttered. It was good to step back sometimes and remember the way things were.

But times change—so do cars—and you learn to adapt. Bud had, and Bud's Grill was a symbol that you could.

What can be difficult to change are perceptions. A 6:00 p.m. live shot in Tarboro? Dear God! But now I pictured Bud rolling up in his old Barracuda with a plate of hot dogs for some bedraggled news reporter once they'd signed off the air. Or maybe pizza burgers. Tarboro it seemed was full of surprises; you just had to dig a little. A girl who found prehistoric remains? You had to keep at it. A man who walked nearly as many miles as the circumference of the earth? Whew. I was tired just thinking about it. Tired and hungry.

Bud heaped my plate with a hot dog and pizza burger both, the burger swimming in sauce and melted cheese—yep, juicy gets me every time. I gripped it with both hands—the thing was enormous—and Bud and Sheila Mae leaned in to watch.

I took as big a bite as my mouth would allow, and the juices rushed in like gas in a bone-dry tank. I raised my eyebrows and nodded, and Bud clapped his hands and beamed, while Sheila Mae laughed so hard she coughed. I tried not to laugh myself, but I ached to tell them just how amazing the burger was and to thank them for their hospitality. And also for reminding me that sometimes perceptions are due for a change.

But all I could manage was a single word. "Good."

WALTER'S GRILL

(AND THE MUSEUM, THE PLANE, AND THE GUN)

THE SIGN SAID "CHICKEN PIE DAY," WHICH WAS MARKED IN BIG blue letters on a white dry-erase board leaning inside the window. I love chicken pie, though I've always called it chicken *pot*pie. I ate it all the time as a kid, especially when my parents went out for the night. Mom would pop a frozen one in the oven while she was getting ready, and when it was done the crust would come out brown and crispy. I'd poke a hole in the dome with my fork and watch the steam pour out before mashing in the crust and swirling it together with the creamy sauce and vegetables. The rich mixture smelled something like melted cheese dunked in warm milk and butter. It gently bubbled in a little tinfoil bowl. I dug in, while Mom stood over me in her pretty dress and glittery necklace. She'd pat the back of my head and smile and did not have to ask how I liked it.

But I did not smile a bit when I read the board in the window of Walter's Grill. I didn't smile because Walter's was supposed to be famous for hot dogs, and my stomach had been growling ever since Robert and I left Raleigh—Robert was the Tar Heel Traveler photographer then. I'd been looking forward to a plump foot-long with extra mustard, maybe two or three. But how were we going to do a hot dog story if everybody in the place was cashing in on the chicken-pie special? I felt like somebody had just poked a hole in my high hopes and mercilessly mashed them in.

Viewers had written me about the dogs at Walter's Grill in Murfreesboro. At first I thought they were talking about the town in Tennessee. A couple fraternity brothers of mine were from Murfreesboro, Tennessee, and it took me four years of college to say the name without tripping on it. But I guess some early settlers to the northeast corner of North Carolina thought it had a nice ring. North Carolina's Murfreesboro is in Hertford County, which I also learned is the home of Chowan University, as in cho-WAHN. At least *Walter's* was easy to say.

The e-mails I'd received about Walter's made the place sound friendly and warm, and all the writers exclaimed over the hot dogs: *Best you'll ever taste!*

Maybe I can eat a hot dog and chicken pie both, I thought. I swished a hand over my belly and remembered Mom patting my head, and my smile returned as I walked into Walter's Grill.

The place was jumping: people eating, the staff hustling, kitchen door swinging open and closed, while the phone on the wall kept ringing. "We're like the local chamber of commerce," said Betsy, who owned Walter's with her husband. "People call here and say, 'Do you know that man who used to own the hardware store? What's his name? Is he still living? Have you got his phone number?' We get calls like that all the time."

Betsy represented the chamber of commerce quite well, I thought. Her blonde hair was fashionably cut. She wore jewelry and makeup and a nice blue shirt. "It's this place," she said, spreading her arms. I looked around and saw people enjoying their chicken pie. "I guess it's our willingness to say, 'Hold on a minute, I'll look up his phone number.' Everybody feels like it's home."

There were four wooden booths against the walls, two red-topped tables in the middle, and an L-shaped counter up front. The six stools were occupied, and the counter crowd had plenty to look at. There must have been half a dozen ladies flipping burgers, slathering hot dogs, chopping chicken, and plopping the tender white chunks into a big pot of simmering sauce.

I might have been drooling, which is maybe why one of the stool sitters threw me a grin. He was an older man with little smiley eyes behind wire-rimmed glasses, the kind of animated expression meant for a TV camera.

"Happy to," he said when I asked about interviewing him. It didn't take long for me to realize his voice was as memorable as his face. "Walter's is all right, sure is," he said in a gravelly baritone.

I learned that Earl was a long-time announcer on the local FM station. I pitched a few other questions and then, what the heck, asked him to give me his best radio voice. Earl cleared his throat and delivered in dramatic fashion. "Sixty-five years of great food, friendly, prompt, smiling service. Walter's Grill, a good place to eat."

> I MIGHT HAVE BEEN DROOLING, WHICH IS MAYBE WHY ONE OF THE STOOL SITTERS THREW ME A GRIN. HE WAS AN OLDER MAN WITH LITTLE SMILEY EYES BEHIND WIRE-RIMMED GLASSES, THE KIND OF ANIMATED EXPRESSION MEANT FOR A TV CAMERA.

Earl was a great find, and I was certain he would not end up on the cutting-room floor. The radio man of Murfreesboro was definitely bound for TV.

Restaurants often boast they have the best hot dogs in North Carolina, or the best burgers, or barbecue, or biscuits. Walter's Grill may have had some or all of the above. But it undoubtedly had the best booths.

Over the years customers had carved their names on the wooden seats and backboards. The wood was dark. Put a knife to it and the carvings popped out. *Cam. Jeb. Dazz. Clay Mac.* People chiseled their names and professed their love with ragged hearts. *Elizabeth loves Moose.*

Walter's opened in 1943, and Lord knows how long people had been digging in. "Lot of names in these booths," said Bill, who introduced himself as Betsy's husband. He was a tall, soft-spoken man with an easy manner. "If they vanish it would be terrible," he said, tracing his finger over the squiggly *t*'s in *Matt.*

He told me several names belonged to people who'd long since passed away. But they weren't forgotten. At Walter's people sat, ordered lunch, and read the booths. "Everybody feels like it's home," Bill said, repeating what Betsy had told me, and apparently Bill and Betsy felt that way, too. They'd owned Walter's for twenty years.

The carvings jogged an idea, a line for my story, and I slid my notepad from my back pocket. *The past is written all over the place*, I wrote with Bill peeking over my shoulder. It turned out Bill was another good spokesperson for the unofficial chamber of commerce. "We've got a lot of history around here," he said. "Murfreesboro's full of history. You been to the Jeffcoat Museum yet?"

Betsy must have overheard because she scooted up beside him. "How about the first plane?" she said. "You know Murfreesboro has the first airplane? And the Gatling gun. Oh, you gotta see that. Do you have time? 'Course you do." She dashed across the floor and reached for the phone, which to my surprise was silent for the moment. How could I object? Bill had asked me how I wanted my hot dogs and was scurrying for the grill to prepare a plate.

Meaty and dripping with mustard! I sat at a stool and devoured two and was contemplating the chicken pie when Betsy began shooshing me out the door. She'd arranged for somebody to meet me at the Jeffcoat Museum around the corner. Jeffcoat was a strange name, I thought, but then this was Murfreesboro, home to Chowan University.

"Oh, you're gonna love it," she said with a shoosh. "Another story." She was talking my language, all right. The more stories, the merrier. But the chicken pie . . .

Five minutes later Robert and I pulled up to a tall brick building with twenty windows across the front. Betsy had told me to look for the old Murfreesboro High School. The impressive exterior was going to make a pretty picture, although we'd agreed to leave the camera in the trunk. It was afternoon already, so for now this was a let's-check-it-out mission. I told Robert we'd make it quick, no problem. *Certainly the museum can't take up the whole building*, I thought and pushed open the front door.

Reporters by nature are generally skeptical, cynical, and rarely fazed, and I suppose that's because they think they've seen it all. But two steps inside the Jeffcoat Museum and my eyes bulged. Forget about being in a hurry. I knew we were going to be here a while.

Music boxes, toasters, tools, china, crystal, plates, pipes, coat hangers, cream-and-sugar containers, salt-and-pepper shakers, and who knows what else were on display, and that was just in the foyer and first room or two.

"We have 997 flatirons," Jimmy Gray said in a proud southern drawl. He was a museum docent with a full head of wavy gray hair. "Feel how heavy that is." He put one of the irons in my hand, and I held on tight for the sake of the polished floor. The thing felt like a forty-pound barbell. Jimmy told me the irons were the type people used on their clothes years ago. "We have the largest collection of flatirons in the United States," he said. "We have the largest collection of wooden washing machines in the United States. And the largest collection of butter churns."

The museum may have had the largest collection of bedpans. They covered an entire wall, hung there like prized artwork, bedpans of every size and shape, although each did come with a prominent hole. I noticed an elegant white one with a pink flower design, and if I hadn't known better I would have set it on my dining room table.

Brady Jeffcoat had accumulated all these items, including scores of mousetraps and BB guns, in fact, every model of Daisy air rifle ever made. "Whatever strikes his fancy, that's what he collects," Jimmy said. The artifacts filled all three floors of the old high school. "He's a very smart man."

Jimmy told me Jeffcoat was in his nineties, an entrepreneur who'd traveled the world but lived in Raleigh and was still collecting. "You ought to see what's in his house," and I thought, *Hmm, another story.*

Jimmy led us through hallways and into rooms filled floor to ceiling; one room was stuffed with stuffed wildlife mounted on every square inch of wall. As we made our way through the building, I admired the elaborate chandeliers that dangled overhead. Jeffcoat collected those, too.

"I've never seen anybody come in here and leave without a smile on their face," Jimmy said. I hated to break the streak, but I was too overwhelmed to smile, and not only that but Jimmy told me we were due across town to see America's first airplane. *America's first airplane?* I thought and wondered if I'd heard him correctly but didn't have the strength to ask. I merely waved good-bye and promised to visit the museum another day with the camera. "Better make it a couple days," he said. "The building's seventeen thousand square feet."

We followed Jimmy's directions to a beige tin box of a place a mile away. The structure could have fit comfortably on the first floor of the Jeffcoat, and so we were feeling brave and opted to lug in the camera. *After all*, I thought, *how many Jeffcoat Museums can there be?*

It was like a warehouse inside, vast and dimly lit, and our footsteps echoed. I made out a tall figure shuffling toward us from the back shadows and hoped we hadn't stumbled upon the dark side of Murfreesboro. But then I noticed the man wore a blue windbreaker, and the next best thing to an interviewee in overalls is a windbreaker-wearing old-timer, particularly when the jacket's faded and spotted with grease. I've found that beneath the fabric are folks who are often salt of the earth.

Sure enough, the tall figure who appeared threw me a toothy grin and stuck out a calloused hand. "Howdy," he said, and I knew we'd come to the right place.

S. T. Wrenn walked us past an old-fashioned buggy, a Model T or Model A maybe, but he didn't give it a glance. We trailed after him through the hollow cavern and came to a winged wooden contraption squatting in the corner. S. T. stopped, hooked his thumbs in the folds of his windbreaker, and poked out his chest. "The first airplane in America," he said.

I squinted at what looked like a wobbly box, dwarfed by a wide thin pair of warped wings. "But what about the Wright brothers?" I said.

"Nope," said S. T. "This un's the first. Thirty years before the Wrights. 'Course it's a replica." He rocked on his big shoes. "Built it ourselves. Just the way it was."

S. T. launched into the story of James Henry Gatling, a Murfreesboro farmer who was fascinated by the buzzards that circled his fields. "And he said he wanted to fly. So that's why they call this the Turkey Buzzard."

S. T. fiddled with one of two black drums attached to the wood frame. "The fan blower," he said, and I winced when he stuck his paw inside, though I'm not sure why. America's first plane looked only a bit more flightworthy than an umbrella. In fact, S. T. told me James Henry once jumped off his barn clutching an umbrella, and I figured he must have ended up with a sore bottom and his neighbors with sore bellies—from laughing. He also experimented with wings made of hay before finally settling on poplar and thin pieces of oak. His Turkey Buzzard was eighteen-feet long with a fourteen-foot wingspan.

On a Sunday afternoon in 1873, the young inventor perched his plane on a twelve-foot-high platform over his cotton gin. He carefully climbed into the cockpit and strapped himself to the chair he'd borrowed from his mother's back porch. A few farmhands leaned against the plane and pushed, while James Henry furiously cranked the handwheel and levers.

The plane took off, the wings caught air, and the good Buzzard glided— proud, majestic, beautiful, according to S. T. "That woulda been something," he said, turning his eyes to the warehouse ceiling. "I'd love to have seen it."

"Well, what happened?" I asked. He had me on the edge of Momma's back-porch seat.

S. T. lowered his head and dug his hands in his pockets. "Flew a hundred feet and crashed into an elm tree at the edge of the yard." It was a moment for the annals of history.

"He had all that stuff figured out before the Wright brothers," S. T. said and began playing with the levers. The wings moved up and down like window blinds. If there'd been some farmhands around, S. T. might have been tempted to take up where James Henry left off.

"That was his one and only flight," he said, slightly out of breath. "Put the plane in storage and spent six years working on it, trying to perfect it, when he died. He never flew again."

"And the plane?" I asked.

"Caught fire a few years later in 1905. There was nothin' left of it." He gazed at the replica. "This is all we have."

I gazed at the replica, too, and cocked my head and thought, *You know, it's not much different from the Wright Flyer photo in all the history books.* "Nobody really knows about James Henry," I said.

"Nobody knows. Schools don't even know." S. T. shook his head but then hooked his thumbs in the folds of his windbreaker again, rocked on his shoes, and poked out his chest. Robert caught him on camera that way, rocking and gazing at the plane, and what a wonderful image it was.

James Henry had a younger brother, Richard, the inventor of the famous Gatling gun. Betsy back at Walter's Grill had scheduled another stop for us, and Robert and I climbed in the car again.

Gene Flowers met us a short distance away at the door of yet another building bulging with hidden history. No windbreaker for him, but he did sport eyeglasses, and I soon realized he was a wise student of Richard Gatling. "He was a farmer," Gene said, escorting us inside and pointing to some old photographs. "He and his father worked on rotary machine equipment."

According to Gene, Gatling remembered that equipment years later as the country marched toward Civil War. "The purpose of inventing the gun was to eliminate deaths, not to cause deaths," Gene said. "It was just, 'I can produce something that will take less man power in the field.'"

I admired Gene's enthusiasm for his subject but couldn't help feeling there was an elephant in the room. One of Gatling's guns, mounted to a metal stand, loomed in the center, a big iron barrel with multiple chambers clamped all around it and a handle jutting from the shaft. "The average soldier could fire one to two rounds a minute," Gene said. "But this gun fired about eight hundred rounds a minute." He cranked the handle, the barrels revolved, and the Gatling gun boomed.

"It's simple when it's put together and you understand how it works," Gene said when he finally quit cranking. "But I'm sure it was very complicated for him to sit there and figure out the mechanics of how to make it work."

"How revolutionary was this?" I asked when my ears stopped ringing.

"Out of the world. Never been heard of or thought of before."

Gene explained how the Gatling gun became a wartime force. Armies used it in war after war all over the world. "They even mounted them on camelback," Gene said, showing me a picture of a camel with the gun secured between its humps.

I noticed Richard Gatling's picture on the wall and thought he appeared quite prominent with his trim white beard, gray suit, and hefty chest. He reminded me of Orson Welles, the filmmaker and actor who directed *The War of the Worlds.*

"Did the gun make him a wealthy man?" I asked.

"It did make him a wealthy man," Gene said. "But he died a pauper."

Gatling died in 1903. Bad investments ruined him, Gene said, and the gun he'd invented to save lives in the end deceived him. "Because it was such a killing machine."

Gene placed his hand on the iron shaft again, and I thought, *Well, I guess we can always use a little more video.* I decided to sacrifice my ears and ask him to crank the handle again. He happily obliged.

We stopped by Walter's Grill on the way out of town, and I thanked Bill and Betsy for the hot dogs and interviews and for the wonderful stories they'd set up for us around town. They smiled warmly, and I said we'd definitely be back another day, a full day just to shoot the Jeffcoat Museum story.

The phone rang then and somebody called, "Order up!" and Bill and Betsy once again sprang into action. The unofficial chamber of commerce never sleeps.

As I turned to go, I made myself a mental note. I would try hard to schedule our next trip to Murfreesboro for a Thursday. Chicken Pie Day!

CENTRAL CAFE

THE E-MAILS KEPT COMING.

Saw your story last night about hot dogs. Well, I got another place for you. . . .

Our hot dog stories were generating lots of feedback. And jealousy. People in towns with hot dog spots we hadn't visited yet were beginning to feel slighted.

We got the best dogs you ever put in your mouth. Promise. Try us!

I knew I was onto something. The hot dogs stories were driving more viewers to the Tar Heel Traveler, but I had to be careful. The series was supposed to showcase colorful people and places across North Carolina, not just hot dogs. I'd trickle in a diner story every couple of weeks and hope the news managers weren't paying attention. I knew how their minds worked. News managers are fickle. They might get a kick out of one, two, or even three hot dogs stories, but then their appetites sour. I found myself torn between satisfying them and the e-mail writers, too.

Same family's been running the place for years. Love nothing more than to see them and their delicious hot dogs featured on the Tar Heel Traveler.

Several notes urged me to visit Central Cafe in Rocky Mount. I think of Rocky Mount as a laid-back town where friendly people tip their hats and help their neighbors, cherish their families, embrace tradition, and enjoy a simple southern life, the kind of people who love watching the *Tar Heel Traveler* and easy-going stories along the back roads. A legendary hot dog diner in Rocky Mount is a temptation hard to ignore.

We rolled up Highway 64, took the ramp toward town, and parked on the street. A red awning rippled over the restaurant entrance, and I pictured the atmosphere inside: folks lounging, sipping cold drinks, and enjoying juicy dogs beneath lazy ceiling fans.

But when I swung open the door, the place was anything but sleepy. Central

Cafe was like Grand Central Station—I meant to scribble that line in my note-pad but people crowded around me and extended their hands. They wanted to meet the TV man from Raleigh and give him a big warm Rocky Mount welcome. All that celebrity can go to your head, except I had a story bouncing around my head and needed to get working on it. There were plenty of people to interview—the tables were full—but who to start with? I was chewing it over when out of the ruckus rose a rhythmic chant.

Run 'em in, run 'em in, ten, twenty, thirty, give me forty!

The would-be auctioneer was a man in a booth, grinning while rat-a-tatting. But—*what's he auctioning?* I wondered, though I didn't much care. I was sold on his enthusiasm and clipped a mic to him even as he rattled on. He never took a breath, not until I waved a hand to ask a question, and when I did, he pounded his fist and shot me his index finger. "Sold to the Tar Heel Traveler!"

Ooh, this is gonna be good, I thought. A colorful interviewee makes for good television. "How're the hot dogs?" I asked.

"You can't eat just one!" he said in a rough sandpapery voice. Too many auctions, I figured, and off he went on another tear, spewing auctionese. We trained the camera on him and let him roll, and I never did find out what started *him* on his roll or if he even really was an auctioneer. But he sure entertained us.

Somebody tugged my arm and pointed to an older man in a brown coat seated in the next booth. "Need to interview him."

I shrugged. "Sure," I said. "Happy to." I should have added, "Thanks!" because the man in the booth turned out to be one of Central Cafe's central pillars. His name was Boot—*Oh, what a terrific name!* And some pretty terrific eyebrows, too, dark and bushy. He'd taken over the place from his father, and now his son ran it. Three generations, a family tradition since 1927. "Put a lot of hours in here," Boot said. And he still was putting in hours, only now coming in most days to relax. He sagged in his booth and sipped his coffee, one of those old-time southern fellows content to keep their thoughts to themselves. But Boot couldn't hide the pride on his face. He smiled ever so slightly but unmistakably.

"WE'VE LIVED ALL OVER THE WORLD," MOM SAID, "AND I CAN PROMISE YOU I HAVE FLOWN HOME STRICTLY FOR A CENTRAL CAFE HOT DOG."

I spotted a woman with two little girls. "One, two, three, four, five," one girl counted, flicking each delicate finger. "I ate five hot dogs!" She flashed a big yellow smile—a kid after my own heart; I guess she liked extra mustard, too.

"We've lived all over the world," Mom said, "and I can promise you I have flown home strictly for a Central Cafe hot dog." She said it like she meant it—she

spoke with a loud strong voice. "I promise you," she repeated and I thought, *Wow, traveling through time zones to eat hot dogs in Rocky Mount.* But I believed her.

"Seven, eight, nine, ten hot dogs!" the little girl squealed and held up her other hand. She said it like she meant it, too, but I'm not sure I believed *her.*

We interviewed several other folks and ate some hot dogs ourselves, and while I don't think I'd ever catch a flight to Central Cafe—international airfare is expensive—I'd definitely make the drive from Raleigh again. Good dogs indeed.

We were just about to leave when the auctioneer dove into his spiel again. I waved from across the room to tell him so long—and to make him stop already. He *did* stop. But instead of pounding the table and shouting, "Sold!" he reached in his jacket pocket, whipped out a little copper bell and waved it back and forth—why he carried a bell with him was another mystery. But I liked the bell; it was catchy. *Like a dinner bell,* I thought. *Ring it and everybody comes.* Sometimes they'll even come from other parts of the world just for a Central Cafe hot dog— or two, three, four . . .

The man grinned and rang and hollered, "Central Cafe just rings my bell!"

PAUL'S PLACE

OCTOBER 19, 2010, WAS A VERY BIG NIGHT. MY FIRST BOOK HAD just been published; this was the day of its official release, and there was a party to celebrate my long-awaited breakthrough. It was in the ballroom of a fancy hotel near Raleigh, and guests dined on heavy hors d'oeuvres and high-dollar cocktails. I sipped on a Diet Coke because I had a speech to make. I was going to read from my book *Tar Heel Traveler: Journeys across North Carolina* and show video clips of the fun stories I'd written about.

The presentation went well. The audio-video equipment worked, and people laughed when they were supposed to. "Anybody have any questions?" I asked at the end. A hand shot up and I nodded. "Yes, Bill," I said. He was a friend of my parents, gray haired and red faced. I liked Bill and felt comfortable enough to call him by his first name. During my speech he'd been among those laughing the hardest.

"Scotty, Scotty," he said. "I've got a story for you!" He scooted to the edge of his chair. "Paul's Place down near Wilmington. Best hot dogs you ever ate. I'd love to take you. My guest, anytime." I thanked him for the invitation and turned to scan the room for other hands, but apparently Bill figured he still had the floor. "Paul's Place," he said. "They got *the best* hot dogs. And let me tell you, that is North Carolina in a nutshell. Little white building on the side of the road. You'd never know it was there." I listened politely but worried about all the question-and-answer time he was eating up. "Oh, you gotta go, hot dogs are out of this world." I finally interrupted and thanked him again and made a show of writing a note to myself at the lectern. "Paul's Place," he said, making sure I had the name right. "Paul's."

Later, I sat and signed copies of my book and wrote little messages on the inside page:

Hope you enjoy these fun NC adventures. There's a great surprise around every bend. Many happy travels!

I realized that night just how much concentration it takes to personalize a book. You have to think of what to write and write it legibly, and by all means spell the person's name correctly, and deal with the pressure to do all that quickly when the line stretches down the hall. I ignored my writer's cramp and plowed ahead.

"Paul's Place!"

My hand jerked, my pen strayed, and a black line went shooting off the *e* at the end of the word *surprise*. I looked up to see Bill standing over me. "Let me take you there, you're gonna love it. Paul's is fantastic. We'll go next week." I had to admit, his description of the place intrigued me, and so did his enthusiasm. He handed me a book to sign and continued to talk on about the great hot dogs and homemade relish. I put my pen to the page and by accident addressed Bill's book with *Dear Paul.*

Weeks passed, and every so often Bill called and asked when I wanted to go. "You busy Friday? How's Friday? How about let's you and me go to Paul's, and bring your cameraman along?"

I glanced at my crowded calendar and sighed. Too many stories to shoot and deadlines to meet. "Can't Friday," I said apologetically. "But soon. I'll let you know."

I did not let him know.

Tar Heel traveling takes concentration, too. It's pull up to a story, hustle in, shoot, interview, bust out, and on to the next one, no lollygagging—well, except maybe to sample a hot dog. Lugging along a third party would slow us down, I thought. And I just couldn't see Bill cramped in the back seat with all those camera lights and extension cords, along with stale Bojangles' coffee cups and food wrappers. So Robert and I shoved off toward Pender County one day without him.

Rocky Point, North Carolina, is barely a spot on the map. The road through town is a highway, but 117 is a sleepy stepsister to Interstate 40. They parallel one another, but I-40 is the quick way to the beach, 117 a long, lonely stretch of asphalt. Paul's Place may have been the only building on that barren road that actually had cars in the parking lot.

We walked into a big room bathed in light from all the windows, and the red-and-white checkerboard floor added to the cheery atmosphere. People sat in wooden booths or stood at the counter at the far end to place their orders. Folks gave us a look but kept at their hot dogs. Maybe they weren't surprised to see a TV camera in Rocky Point. But a TV camera in Rocky Point? I was surprised they weren't surprised.

I looked for Paul, having no idea what Paul looked like. When a slow-moving man shuffled up, heaved a sigh, and muttered, "Hey, how ya'll doin'?" I thought it was just some happy Joe who'd stuffed himself silly and needed a nap. But Joe turned out to be David, and David turned out to be Paul.

"David Paul," he said.

"Are you the owner?" I asked.

"That's me," he said in a slow southern drawl, and I thought I saw his gray eyes sparkle. But he still looked like he could use a rest, and I suggested we sit a while.

Running a restaurant is hard work—that, too, takes concentration, not to mention commitment—and David Paul had poured his heart and mind into Paul's Place, as his family had before him.

"My grandfather came here in 1928," he said and pointed to a snapshot of a blurry figure beneath an Esso sign.

"He made hot dogs at the gas station?" I asked.

David answered by pointing to a second snapshot and another blurry figure. "My father," he said. "He was cooking himself some hot dogs one day at my grandfather's Esso. Somebody walked in and said, 'Give me one of those. How much are they?' Daddy said, 'Oh, throw a nickel in the cup.'" A smile crept along David's lips. "That's the way it started," he said. "And it has stayed in the family."

We chatted a while longer, and maybe David wasn't so weary after all. I think laid-back was just the way he was, content and stress-free—the man would have no problem at all signing books with a line out the door. He was about the same age as Bill, and I was thinking the two of them could talk all day.

We stood, and David introduced me to his son, J. P., who was cooking behind the counter. J. P. told me how proud he was to carry on the tradition. I asked him about his dad. "He's a good man," J. P. said and winked. "He's made a few hot dogs in his lifetime."

I turned to a round-bellied man in a booth with two loaded ones on a plate. "What is it about the hot dogs?" I asked.

"I think it's the relish."

"The relish?" His answer surprised me.

"The relish is the key. That's what's made the place famous."

THE RELISH IS THE KEY. THAT'S WHAT'S MADE THE PLACE FAMOUS.

It was then I noticed Paul's Special Relish at every table, bottled in fat Mason jars with red, white, and blue labels. I learned the Paul family had been making it for years without divulging the ingredients.

"It's hard to find that flavor," a lady told me. "Mmm, mmm," she murmured.

"I think Paul's is about history and tradition," said a man in a UNCW shirt. It turned out, he was the university's baseball coach and most days drove from UNC-Wilmington to Rocky Point just to eat a dog. "My first encounter with Paul's was when I was eighteen years old. Eighteen! And now I'm sixty-six, so you do the math."

I calculated—forty-eight years. Forty-eight years!

Before leaving Paul's Place I sampled a hot dog smothered with Paul's Special Relish. I'm not normally a relish eater, but after finishing the dog I sprang for a couple of fat Mason jars to carry home.

Robert and I stepped into the hot sun just as another car pulled up. A man with a big smile and floppy T-shirt jumped out and threw me a hearty, "Hello!" I couldn't resist and reached for the microphone again.

"Heading to the beach?" I asked.

"Heading to the beach."

"And had to stop at Paul's?"

"Had to. It's kinda in the middle of nowhere, but it's known all over the place. I tell you, they've got it down, and it's good. Worth the trip to come get a Paul's Place hot dog."

I was glad I hadn't rushed past him without stopping—maybe David had taught me something about slowing down. The man's interview would make a nice end to my story. "Can't beat it," he said.

Robert and I rolled on toward Wilmington; we had other stories to shoot. Along the way I tried to scratch out a Paul's Place script on my notepad, but every time we hit a bump my pen skittered across the page, leaving scraggly lines of black ink where they weren't supposed to be. I thought of Bill.

I thought of him scrunched in the back seat with lights and extension cords on his lap, relish on his cheeks and a satisfied grin slathered across his face. He would have loved it, would love to have been there with us, talking to folks, listening to David's story—which he probably already knew by heart—soaking it all in: the place, the dogs, the relish. I'm sure Bill wanted me in on the secret, not what was in the relish inside the jar but what was in the people inside the building. That was the story he'd been trying to tell me all along.

Regret. I suppose it comes with the television territory—the missed stories and skipped interviews. And how I wished I'd called Bill before traveling to Paul's Place.

I did call him later to let him know we'd made the trip and to watch for the story when it aired. I left the message on his answering machine. Bill wasn't there.

But he was there in my story. I pictured him standing over me again when I sat down at my desk later to write it. I think I wrote it the way he would have liked, full of warmth and character, capturing the friendliness of the people and sincerity of their feelings.

When Robert edited the piece, he packed it with shots of hot dogs and relish and, man, we both were ready for a return trip. And maybe a couple more Mason jars, too.

This time I'd make sure Bill came along.

CAPT'N FRANKS

ORVILLE AND WILBUR WRIGHT CARRIED SHOTGUNS AND BLASTED away, but not at people. They shot mice.

POW!

The Outer Banks was a barren strip of land in 1903, and I can only imagine the Wright brothers must have been half nuts traveling all the way from their home in Ohio to concoct some crazy experiments at the edge of the earth. A flying machine? What the heck was that? Kill Devil Hills? What in the world was there?

Nothing was there, except wind and sand and two starry-eyed brothers and the little shack they threw together to live in. They actually tar-papered the roof wearing button-down shirts and bow ties. I've seen a grainy photograph of Wilbur in church clothes dragging a grimy sheet across the sand. Another picture shows Orville, also neatly dressed, cleaning his rifle. There *was* something on the Outer Banks back then: mice.

POW!

It was one of those beautiful summer days in Kitty Hawk, low eighties with an Outer Banks breeze. Capt'n Franks was easy to spot, a tall building with a towering sign out front. But what struck me was the Volkswagen in the parking lot. The bug in the end space was sunny yellow with a wiry hot dog man painted on the door. The caricature wore oversize sneakers and white gloves and snapped his fingers while dancing a jig. The car was a convertible, which seemed appropriate. On the Outer Banks, folks tend to let their hair fly.

I walked into a room full of sandy flip-flops, and though it was barely noon, many a tanned arm was lifting a longneck. The Doobie Brothers crooned from hidden speakers, and a bright row of pastel hats dangled from an overhead wire. Another wire stretched above the lunch counter. The blonde girl running the register stood on tiptoe, reached up, grabbed the wire, and clamped a paper ticket to it with a clothespin. "Two Junkyards!" she shouted and snapped the order down the line to the cook at the other end. I had no idea what two Junkyards were but would have eaten them just because I loved the clothespin system they'd rigged. The cute blonde was impressive, too.

To me Capt'n Franks felt like a little Disneyland, a loud, crowded, colorful place brimming with happy energy. Everybody seemed to be on vacation. At one table a group of young guys and girls in T-shirts clinked Coronas. "Cheers!"

I also noticed plenty of families. A dad in a booth punched a video game on his cell while Mom tucked her little boy's napkin in his lap and cut his hot dog into tiny pieces. Well, at least Dad was on vacation anyway.

I soon met Harvey Hess. And Harvey Hess. Harvey and Harvey were father and son and the "captains" of Capt'n Franks. "You know, I didn't go to day care or anything like that," said the younger Harvey, who by then had graduated from college but still could have passed for a fraternity house president—or social chairman. He showed me a snapshot taken when he was a toddler, propped in what looked like an inflatable high chair with OSCAR MAYER written across the front of it. He wore a little red Santa Claus hat with a white pom-pom, and the camera had caught him in mid giggle. "I just came here every day," he said, and I guessed that meant even at Christmas. He was still here and still smiling twenty-some years later. "It's fast paced," he said, and with that he was gone, off to clean a table or help with an order, which left me with the older Harvey and a feeling of synchronicity. It seemed to me Kitty Hawk had laid claim to yet another successful tandem.

"My granddad bought the property in the early '60s," said the gray-haired Harvey. "Back when there was nothing here." *But there was something here,* I thought and coughed to camouflage my chuckles. *Mice!*

"Fish," Harvey said. "Dad loved to fish."

Harvey told me that on one of those fishing trips to the Outer Banks his dad thought, "Hey, why not build a hot dog stand?" Capt'n Franks wobbled to

TO ME CAPT'N FRANKS FELT LIKE A LITTLE DISNEYLAND, A LOUD, CROWDED, COLORFUL PLACE BRIMMING WITH HAPPY ENERGY. EVERYBODY SEEMED TO BE ON VACATION. AT ONE TABLE A GROUP OF YOUNG GUYS AND GIRLS IN T-SHIRTS CLINKED CORONAS. "CHEERS!"

life in 1975, almost three-quarters of a century after the Wright brothers' first flight—and there was still nothing there.

"There was nothing on this road for about two miles in either direction," Harvey said, waving a hand at Highway 12. We'd slipped outside to the seating area, which he seemed proud to show off, especially the big Adirondack-type chairs. "Now look at it." The chairs were purple, but I think he meant the highway and all the businesses crowding the asphalt. Harvey shouted over the traffic. "Like this guy from Michigan told me the other day, when he got in his car he put Capt'n Franks in his GPS and that's how he traveled here, all the way from Michigan right to Capt'n Franks."

The pie-in-the-sky idea had become a landmark. In fact, I was willing to bet a couple Junkyards that more people visited Capt'n Franks than the nearby Wright Brothers National Memorial. The place had taken off.

"People from all over the world have come here," Harvey said, walking me back inside and tapping his finger on a picture of country singer Johnny Cash cuddling a pretty blonde in front of the restaurant. Johnny Cash liked to fish, too, and I almost joked about his nice catch when Harvey told me the blonde was his wife—Harvey's wife, not Johnny's.

He showed me another photo, one of a scowling John McEnroe. The bad boy of tennis looked like he'd either just lost a match or balled out the ump. He wore a long-sleeve T-shirt, and Harvey pointed to the writing along Johnny Mac's arm: BEST HOT DOGS ON THE BEACH. "He's wearing one of ours," Harvey said and beamed.

"I tell you, I'd have a revolution on my hands if I tried to change this place," he said, and I watched him track a ticket zipping down the wire. "It's always been about the hot dog. I mean, it's just always been about the dog."

He turned to mingle with folks piling in, everybody in shorts and T-shirts with happy smiles and sunburns or deep tans and whiskers. "Come in, come in," Harvey said. He stood near the entrance by a dry-erase board where somebody had written LEAVE ALL GRUMPS OUTSIDE.

I probably could have picked any table in the place, and the people sitting there would have happily agreed to an interview. Why not? They were on vacation. It'd be fun. I chose the longest, rowdiest table of the bunch, one with guys slugging beer. "He'll do it, he'll do it," nine out of ten of them said when I approached, all pointing to the big man at the head of the table. I saw the fella look at his empties and weigh whether he was up to it.

"Sure," he said at last. "Nobody who knows me is gonna see this anyway. I'm from Cleveland!" I didn't tell him the story would end up on WRAL.com and that people around the globe could access it.

The Cleveland man turned out to be quite a character. The place had him jazzed, and he raved about how great it was. "I've had two of the Junkyard dogs, and they were worth every cent and every bite," he said, wagging a meaty finger at the camera. "It's described as the works, and I promise you it is the works." His buddies hooted and egged him on.

Cleveland told me this was his first visit to Capt'n Franks, and I think maybe that offered him some perspective. "Look at this," he said, pointing his thumb at a framed photo on the wall behind him. The picture was a washed-out aerial image of sky and sand and one little building and nothing else. "That's what it looked like when it first opened, just a stand-alone place. And it's endured all these years." Cleveland turned back to the camera. "That's amazing," he said. "Amazing."

I felt like clinking a longneck with him after hearing those articulate words. Or maybe it was just the atmosphere that had *me* jazzed. I felt I was on vacation, too. And again, there was that odd feeling of synchronicity. The man was from Ohio and so were Wilbur and Orville. And if that wasn't enough I stumbled into a second Ohioan at another table.

He was a bronze-skinned man with a bushy mustache who told me he'd been coming to the Outer Banks since 1972. "And I been driving the same car down here every year. That's forty years," he said. "You seen that Chevy in the parking lot? Can't miss it."

I hadn't seen it but was dying to take a look. I figured a rig like that deserved a place next to the Wright Flyer at the Smithsonian.

I interviewed a college kid with his girlfriend who told me he collected Capt'n Franks T-shirts and had about fifteen of them. "One for every year I've been coming here," he said and squeezed his girlfriend's hand. I had a feeling he'd be buying two on this visit.

I finally had a chance to play the vacationer myself and shoved my notepad in my back pocket, settled on a stool at the end of the counter, and told the cook, "Gimme a Junkyard. Why not?" Sometimes you gotta push the envelope.

I tried to relax like everybody else, but my mind kept mulling the story. Who was I fooling? I was still working even when I wasn't working—though I did do some looking. The blonde was reaching for the wire and, man, was she a cutie-pie. I thought I'd better look elsewhere and caught sight of that old aerial photo on the wall. *Why on earth had Harvey's dad erected his hot dog building in the* middle of nowhere? I wondered. *The man must have had incredible foresight. Just like the Wright brothers.*

POW!

The clothespin smashed against the end of the wire directly above my head, and I jumped. The cook grinned. He reached up and snatched the ticket and a moment later slid me a plate with my hot dog, which lay hidden beneath a pile of chili and slaw. I grinned back and opened wide. Half the Junkyard ended up on my cheeks—but then, magnificent creations are often messy.

I wore my smile into the parking lot where I spotted that forty-year-old Chevy, a real rust bucket with a faded Capt'n Franks sticker in the rear window. And it occurred to me that here was yet another Kitty Hawk pairing. The rust bucket and the restaurant were both still truckin'.

But it was the bright yellow bug I liked best, especially the hot dog man on the door. I felt like dancing a jig myself even with the Junkyard lying heavy on my belly. I would love to have taken a spin and let my hair fly. Because after all, that's what the Outer Banks is all about—flying, pushing the envelope, sticking your neck out, and letting the wind blast away.

POW!

WHY ON EARTH HAD HARVEY'S DAD ERECTED HIS HOT DOG BUILDING IN THE MIDDLE OF NOWHERE? I WONDERED. THE MAN MUST HAVE HAD INCREDIBLE FORESIGHT. JUST LIKE THE WRIGHT BROTHERS.

Directly behind WRAL is Cloos' Coney Island, known for hot dogs and fountain drinks with crushed ice. I occasionally meet my wife, Nina, there for lunch. I slip out the back door of the TV station, walk past the gardens, across the shopping center parking lot, and I'm there, three minutes max. I'm usually late.

Dan owns Cloos', and he always gives a big wave when I walk in. He's a huge Tar Heel Traveler fan. "Where you headin' this week?" he says.

He also loves the Detroit Red Wings, and in that sense we're part of the same ice hockey brotherhood. I still play hockey once a week in a men's league. All three of my kids play, and I routinely pick up free tickets to Carolina Hurricanes games; WRAL has its own suite near center ice.

Nina likes the gyros at Cloos', and I usually order a cheeseburger. I'm saving up for a Cloos' hot dog when I do a story on the place. I *should* do a story on Cloos'. It deserves a story. It's been around a long time, the food's good and customers loyal. A lady named Sandy I know from church meets friends at Cloos' almost every day.

"That's a story right there," Nina says, pointing her head at the ladies gathered around a table marked RESERVED FOR CLOOS' CLUB. Sandy and her friends always sit at the *same* table. "They'd be great," Nina says, and I know

they *would* be great. Sandy herself has one of those twinkly-eyed faces that light up a lens. Include some other regulars, Dan, and the sports memorabilia on the walls and I'd have a memorable hot dog story. Besides that, I liked Dan. I *wanted* to do a story on Cloos'.

But I could still hear my old news director from Dayton, Ohio huffing in my head, "Convenient interview." He frowned upon stories that were too easy to get.

"Delicious," Nina says, chewing her gyro. The cheeseburger hits the spot, too. Cloos' also has good french fries. They're skinny, and Nina and I always share an order.

I look around at the hockey signs and NC State posters and ESPN playing on the overhead TV, and I think of the news director I have now. *Would he scoff at my "convenient interview"?* Half the newsroom eats at Cloos'.

I hear the ladies behind me, giddy as schoolgirls. "You really should do a story," Nina says, and I nod my head, yes. Yes, I will do a story on Cloos'. Sometime. Sometime soon. I'm sure I will. Someday.

Maybe.

CITY LUNCH
CAFE

JESUS PRAYED IN THE WINDOW. HE WORE A LONG ROBE AND KNELT by a rock, his hands tightly clasped, peering toward heaven. It was a big pane of glass, and the poster took up most of it. Printed in bold red letters on the right-hand side was JESUS CHRIST OUR LORD AND SAVIOR. And written at the top of the poster: CITY LUNCH.

I stood across the street from City Lunch Cafe and noticed other signs, too—indications of hard times: lots of empty storefronts in downtown Franklinton. But that's what drew me to the little town north of Raleigh. People had written me about City Lunch, how special it was, a gathering spot, and how the family who ran it had struggled to keep the place open. *This sour economy sure is taking a toll*, read one of the notes. *Won't you come do a story? Please? Such good Christian folks.*

The best hot dog places aren't just about hot dogs but about people, their dedication and nose-to-the grindstone work ethic, and their trials and tribulations along the way. City Lunch sounded like it had all the right ingredients, just a humble place on South Main with a gray awning and that big plate-glass window. But I must admit, Jesus had me a little intimidated.

I walked into a packed house, and oohs and aahs rippled through the room. "The TV people from Raleigh! That's them! Look!" I thought one lady might tumble out of her booth. Her eyes grew as big as hamburger buns, and her own buns squirmed. Celebrities had come to town! The awestruck onlookers had me a little intimidated, too.

I nodded and smiled and took in the surroundings, and it didn't take long to feel as though I'd stepped into a classic mom-and-pop diner. Even the lay-out was typical: booths along the left wall, a not-quite-wide-enough center aisle, red-cushioned stools to the right beneath a long counter, and beyond it a much-too-narrow corridor running alongside the grill, fridge, ice machine, drink machine, and who knows what else crammed against the wall.

No fewer than five City Lunch staffers jostled up and down that sliver of space, bumping elbows and rear ends while hoisting plates full of hot dogs and hamburgers high over their heads. I noticed one fussbudget in particular shouting orders. "Hamburger! Put on another hamburger!"

I NODDED AND SMILED AND TOOK IN THE SURROUNDINGS, AND IT DIDN'T TAKE LONG TO FEEL AS THOUGH I'D STEPPED INTO A CLASSIC MOM-AND-POP DINER.

"Oh, that's just Sharon," said a man in a booth with a gray handlebar mustache in an accent from north of the Mason-Dixon. Tony said folks in Franklinton had welcomed him when he moved south, especially the kind people at City Lunch. "Lot of camaraderie, lot of friendship, lot of love," he said. "Everybody's friendly—well, except for Sharon." The words had barely left his lips when a balled-up napkin zinged past our camera and hit him smack in the head. Tony laughed so hard I thought he might tumble out of the booth, too.

"Don't believe nothin' they say. They're lying!" Sharon's shrilly voice touched off some chuckles, but people kept right on eating. I think they'd heard it before.

Sharon was a skinny freight train in motion, carrying plates, juggling drinks, taking money, making change, always moving, and often tooting that shrill whistle. "Hot dog! Gimme a hot dog!" She reminded me of Granny from the *Beverly Hillbillies* TV show, a feisty old biddy, only Sharon was tall as a sign post with blonde curly hair cut short and tight. She was probably in her late sixties—but since she might read this, I'll say early forties.

"It's like one big happy family," said a lady at a table, and it felt that way to me, too, like a big happy family crowded around a good hot meal with pictures and posters and whatnots on the walls, and plenty of joking, shoulder patting, and handshaking. "Good to see you, good to see you."

"I got three hot dogs, two hamburgers, two french fries," said a man spread across one side of a booth. "I'm gonna do something to it, you know what I mean?"

His name was Wilbur, and he could have been the poster child of a mom-and-pop regular: red T-shirt under blue jean overalls and a John Deere hat perched high on his round head. He talked like any one of the Beverly Hillbillies in a classic slow southern drawl, chock-full of mischievous wit. "I always been big, but I don't call it fat. I call it blessed with gravitational pull, you know

what I mean?" Wilbur's chubby cheeks swelled with a huge grin, but my own grin might have been wider. He'd given me the best sound bite of the day, maybe the year.

I shook hands with Clyde, who owned City Lunch, a soft-spoken man who also pastored a church in town. "This is the sixty-fourth year we've been here," Clyde said, and he told me about his mom and dad buying the place in 1949. Their picture hung near the door, and they looked like such a nice couple, dressed in their fine church clothes, seated close and posing for the camera. But it was tough running a business, Clyde said, especially in recent years with stores closing and the high school moving away. His folks were gone now, and he'd wondered about moving on. "But it's family," he said, "and you can't sell your family."

My eyes popped when Clyde told me his family included Sharon. *Clyde married to Sharon?* I pinched the bridge of my nose—maybe he'd think some stray grease had splattered me. But yes, Clyde and Sharon. And their grown daughter, Michelle, had spent *her* years at City Lunch. Michelle wore a colorful tie-dyed City Lunch T-shirt, and I watched her slice a hunk of chocolate pecan cobbler. "People love her desserts," Clyde said.

Customers kept tugging my elbow and whispering in my ear. They told me Clyde and Sharon had helped so many people down on their luck and given folks free meals even when they were struggling themselves. I thought of Jesus and loaves and fishes. "Clyde is the sweetest man you'll ever wanna know," said a woman who then raised her voice and one of her french fries. "They have *the best*!" she said. "So crispy!"

"What about Sharon?" I asked.

"Oh. Well, she's nice, too," she said and laughed.

A woman named Alta introduced herself. She had gray hair and a pleasant smile, though her eyes seemed to water a bit. "That's the stool he always sat on," she said. The stool she pointed to was empty. "My husband was killed a few years ago in an automobile wreck on Number 1 Highway, and for about fifty years he came here every morning and had breakfast." Alta perked up when she said she'd become a regular herself. "Yes sir, every chance I get."

"We've done a lot of ministry through this store," Clyde said in his gentle way and cast a glance down the counter. Alta had grabbed a rag and was wiping the tabletop. "Good to see her smiling again," he said. "She's a help to us, too." But I suspect it worked both ways. I think City Lunch was a help to Alta, her sanctuary. Jesus was in the window, and her friends were all around. And maybe her husband didn't seem so far away either.

"Hamburger!" Sharon cried. "Put on another hamburger!"

Okay, I thought with a sigh. *Time to step in front of the freight train.*

"Why do people poke fun at you?" I asked Sharon and flinched, expecting her to hurl another napkin. But she merely slapped the air and drummed her lips.

"You know Rodney Dangerfield?" she said, and I nodded. He'd been a popular standup comedian whose famous tag line Sharon delivered on cue: "I don't get no respect." But I detected a trace of a smile when she said it. The irony was that people loved Rodney Dangerfield. And they loved Sharon. "Two hot dogs!" she hollered.

I enjoyed my two dogs with extra mustard. "Get you anything else?" Sharon asked.

"Piece of cake?" Michelle added.

"Sure enjoyed having you," said Clyde.

It was Alta who opened the door for me. "Hurry back," she said.

I turned to face her. "I will," but I'd already crossed the threshold and found myself speaking instead to Jesus in the window. I admired his long robe, the large rock, his hands clasped, peering toward Heaven. "Thank you!" I said—to them both.

JONES LUNCH
(AND THE ROAD RUNNERS
AND ELMER FUDD)

A STANDUP IS AN EASY THING: MEMORIZE A COUPLE SENTENCES, look at the lens, and recite your lines. News directors love it when their reporters appear on camera. Love it even more when they walk and talk and point and gesture. Action, they want action! Ratings, they want ratings!

"Anytime," Robert said. He hovered over the camera, which was propped on a tripod thirty feet away, while I got ready to announce my spiel. I was about to play Mr. Casual, strolling the sidewalk in front of Jones Lunch in downtown Clayton. We'd spent the past ninety minutes inside, collecting a pile of fun interviews and capturing the cozy, country flavor of the place. I loved the atmosphere and energy of Jones. Folks were having a ball, laughing and grinning and kicking back like they were all fast friends and fond neighbors.

We had ourselves another great diner piece. All that remained was our routine way of introducing stories, a quick opening standup. And after that, maybe a dog or two with extra mustard.

I stepped toward Robert and started in: *Believe it or not, we move pretty fast in our Tar Heel travels, jumping from one story to . . .*

I stopped midsentence and midstride, take one busted.

I'm usually good about nailing standups on first takes. I've watched other reporters repeatedly flub theirs and witnessed fed-up photographers grow purple in the face and eat their hats. But my concentration wasn't there this time. My mind had clouded over. I stood stock-still in a dense fog under the bright sun.

I'm sure Robert noticed my gaze drifting into the distance. He straightened and glanced behind him in a what-the-heck's-he-lookin'-at motion. Traffic puttered along Main just like always, and he swung back and studied me with a squint. He was probably hungry for two all the way and itching to get a move on. But for me, the homey feel of Jones Lunch had already begun to unravel like a slippery roll of film. A little movie played inside my head, and though I should have shrugged it away, I couldn't help myself. I was like a highway rubbernecker who crawls past the car wreck, ogling for a glimpse. Jones Lunch had set the movie in motion. It was one I'd already seen.

I'd been here before, on this same street at another time on another story with another photographer, and my mind had picked this moment to punch rewind. The gears turned. The film slithered through my memory reel. And just like that, it all flashed back with a burst.

Thwack!

June 2002

The door burst open, thwacking the side of the building, and three wild-eyed muscle men crashed out and scampered around the corner in front of me. All three slipped on some gravel and nearly fell, and I bit my lip to keep from laughing. They reminded me of the Road Runner TV cartoon when Road Runner whips his little legs around like a high-speed windmill before finally gaining traction.

But something told me this was no laughing matter.

I was covering general news back then, a story about a furniture store that had burned and was reopening, and I'd been getting ready to go live on our noon news.

I was working with Courtney that day, a young female photographer who'd parked the satellite truck at a gas station across from the furniture store. Courtney was slender but strong—you've got to be tough to lug that heavy camera around all day. She'd snapped a rubber band around her brown hair and wore a loose T-shirt and cargo pants with pockets and loops up and down the legs. She was standing by the truck's open side door, gripping the telephone and griping with master control to hurry up and tune in the shot, while I paced and rehearsed my lines.

A convenience store stood just beyond the edge of the parking lot, and I happened to be facing it when—*thwack!* Talk about discombobulating my concentration. I quit biting my lip and stood slack jawed as the three brutes scurried past.

I knew it was serious when an older gentleman staggered out behind them clutching a rag to his head. "I robbed," he cried in broken English. "Stop 'm." The rag was spotted with blood.

"Stop 'm!"

January 2010

I'd long ago tossed that bloody rag in the corner of my mind—it had been eight years—but now it came whirling back, the bloody thing fluttering behind my eyes. The convenience store was just a block from Jones Lunch.

Robert waved a hand. "Okay," he said, and I shook like a wet dog, rolled my head around my neck, and started in on standup take two:

Believe it or not, we move pretty fast in our Tar Heel travels, jumping from one story to the next. But fast does not mean fast food. . . .

I drew a blank on the next line. It was gone, poof, out the door and around the corner. So much for take two.

———

"Oh, you're gonna love this place," Robert had said when we pulled up to Jones Lunch. He lived in Clayton and knew the place well. And yet I couldn't help stealing a look down the street, picturing the old man and the roughnecks peeling past me. Eight years and I didn't know whether to laugh or tremble. I was still toiling it over when we pushed through the door of Jones Lunch.

The place may have been known for hot dogs, but I felt like I'd stepped into an Italian cafe. It must have been the red-and-white tablecloths, people sitting close together in a big noisy room, and the spicy aroma that hovered like a doughy cloud. Several black poles stood like steel sentinels holding up the ceiling, which made the place feel old and rustic and warm and snug at the same time.

I found owner Curtis Jones behind the counter, wrapped in a white apron. He had a gray beard and mustache, and a tangle of hair stuck out from under his black ball cap. The grill hissed and spat, and Curtis kept turning from me to it, rolling the dogs and tipping his cap, trying hard to be polite without burning the profits. His mom and dad had started Jones Lunch more than half a century before. He pointed his spatula at their photo on the far wall, Mom and Dad at the grill, both with dark-rimmed glasses and smiles for the camera.

Curtis told me his parents had passed on, but the restaurant was alive and well. He threw another bundle of dogs on the grill, which blistered and sizzled. I told him I'd come back when the crowd calmed down and he had time to talk. "Don't worry about us," I said, pointing a thumb over my shoulder. "We got lots of folks to talk to." He waved his spatula. Have at it, the spatula said.

I took a moment to survey the room—every table was full—and I thought, *Man, this is great.* And it's that thought I tucked in my head for later. For the opening standup:

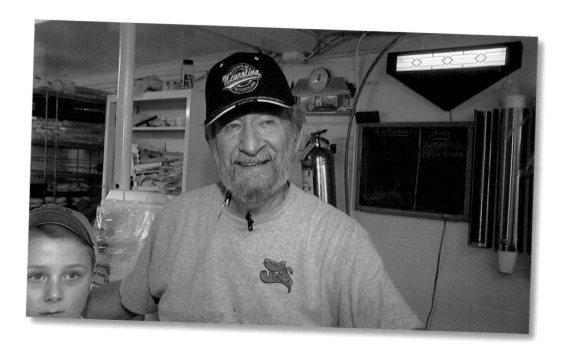

Oh, we love a great old local lunch spot. . . .

I stopped midsentence again—take three, kaput—and though Robert hadn't taken a bite of his hat yet, we were wasting a lot of tape. He'd kept the camera rolling. And my little film reel upstairs kept rolling, too.

The three men ran between the store they'd robbed and the gas station we'd adopted for our live shot. I watched them hustle toward a dirt road that sloped past the back of the buildings. The path was steep, and they kicked up a cloud of dust and stones, and I thought if they aren't careful they're going to tumble head over heels. I hustled to the crest of the hill to watch, and that's when I spotted a car parked at the bottom. *Man,* I thought, *I gotta pay attention to this.*

The car was dark blue, or maybe green, some plain old-model type. The hoodlums slammed into the side of it, threw open the doors and clambered in, bumping each other and flopping onto the seats.

The way the car was pointed I figured they'd come tearing past the back of the gas station and out the other side. The other side—Courtney was by the live truck parked near the other side of the lot. Not only that, but she had her camera.

I backed up fast. "They've robbed the place!" I cried, hoping she heard me. "Shoot 'em!" I shouted, hoping the hoodlums heard me, too.

News photographers are generally quick on their feet. It's shoot first, think later. A puzzled look crossed her face for just a second before she heaved the camera onto her shoulder. I pointed at the other end of the gas station and ran, and that's when I noticed another road directly ahead that led up the slope and fed onto Main Street.

I slammed on the foot brakes and so did Courtney. She crouched and suctioned one eye to the lens. I was sure the car would come barreling into view, and as I waited, tomorrow's headline screeched across my brain: WRAL News Crew Snags Would-Be Thieves! I almost laughed again, but then I saw Courtney teeter. She'd crouched too long. *Where are they?* We both stood and jogged another few strides and cleared the building. And my breath caught in my throat. I saw nothing but open land below.

The car was nowhere in sight.

Believe it or not, we move pretty fast in our Tar Heel travels. . . .

But not fast enough, I thought, crunching the brakes on standup take four. *C'mon*, I told myself, *concentrate. Jeez Louise.*

The hoodlums had outsmarted me. *Shoulda moved quicker*, I thought, *shoulda run past the building and caught the license plate.* But it was too late now. And why dawdle on those three stooges anyway? The clowns were spoiling my story on Jones Lunch. And I definitely had the makings of a great story.

———

I spotted one long table in the center of the restaurant with people elbow to elbow, gray-haired folks and a fuzzy-headed baby and toddler. They ate and laughed and chitchatted away. But one voice rose above the others.

A little old lady sat at the head of the table, but she was not the kind with knitting needles and an afghan. This one was loud and animated. She reminded me of Frank Perdue, the chicken executive whose TV ads in the '70s made him a national celebrity. It helped that Frank Purdue looked like a chicken, beak faced and wrinkly. He spoke through his nose but talked good old-fashioned common sense, and people trusted him.

This lady looked like Frank Perdue, but in a good way. She was cute and feisty and shared that same whiney twang and folksy wit. "Don't you go gettin' fresh with me," she said when I asked her to slip the mic cord under her shirt, but she winked when she said it. Then she introduced me to the table.

"This is my friend Alice and her husband and great nephew, and . . ." She flapped a hand at the rest. "And I don't really know the other people." The table broke out in hoots and cackles until her twang quieted the clamor.

"If you haven't had a Jones hot dog, you've never had a hot dog. If you've never met at Jones with your friends, you don't have any friends." The table burst into laughter again, and I thought, *Man, she's fantastic.* Better yet, she'd loosened up everyone else at the table, too.

"A hot dog with chili, slaw, extra mustard, and half an order of fries," piped Ginger, bobbing her head with each ingredient. "And sweet tea!" She was a country girl who'd grown up with Jones Lunch and most days ordered the same lunch. "You come in here and you always see somebody you know. It's like coming home."

I thought about staying at the table and interviewing everybody around it. Easy schmeezie. But I felt obligated to venture outside the comfort zone. If there was one thing I'd learned in Clayton it was to always take another step.

"I used to bag groceries here," said a T-shirted man in a booth by the cinderblock wall.

"Groceries?"

"Yeah, used to be a grocery store. Opened as a restaurant in 1958, and I been eatin' here ever since." He looked down at the mustardy remnants on his plate. "Just goes to show hot dogs are good for you."

"This is the place to come for lunch," said a woman with two young daughters.

"Takes you back a few years," said an older man, holding his grandchild.

I was piling up sound bites but took a moment to look around and search for ideas to drop in my story. I spotted a metal sign that read Coca Cola Ave and a sheet of notebook paper taped to the wall where somebody had written Jones Is Good. A miniature hot dog man waved a meaty thumb in the air, and I flipped open my pad and scribbled my own clever caption: *Thumbs up for Jones Lunch!*

"Has it changed at all?" I finally had a chance to interview Curtis behind the counter.

"We've changed nothing."

"What would your folks think of Jones Lunch today?" I asked.

"I think they'd be proud of it."

"You think they'd want to order a hot dog?"

"I'm sure they'd eat one if they could." Curtis gave the camera a beautiful chuckle, nice, warm, and homey.

The story was just about wrapped. A few exterior shots and an opening standup and we'd be done. Robert and I slipped outside.

And it all came back. Déjà vu in downtown Clayton.

———

No car, just an empty field. I could hear Courtney breathing hard, or maybe it was my heart thumping in my ears. The men had evidently peeled straight ahead while we'd waited for them to roar up the side. The adrenaline ran out of me like water and my shoulders sagged. The Road Runners had gotten away, stolen the last laugh. I felt like Elmer Fudd.

And then I saw Courtney running again, and I mean really sprinting, full out, and the adrenaline whooshed right back in. She was running for the live truck. I checked my watch. One minute till noon.

All things considered, my live shot about the furniture store went okay. I was younger then with a sharp memory and no way was I going to let three roughnecks rattle me. The police didn't rattle me either. While I spoke on camera about the store rising from the ashes I saw two officers out of the corner of my eye talking to the man with the rag at his head.

After the live shot the police talked to me, too, and I told them what I could, but by then the details were already beginning to blur. Maybe my memory wasn't so good after all.

As soon as I could I called the newsroom and described what had happened in dramatic, play-by-play fashion. My adrenaline was flying again. I made sure to mention the bloody rag right away. "Anybody die?" the honchos wanted to know. "Rushed to the hospital?" When I told them no, they said skip it.

"But . . ."

"Forget about it. Whatchya got for us at five and six o'clock? Whatever you got, you're live, definitely live."

<hr>

Robert waved his hand again, but I barely noticed. My eyes floated down the block, and I half expected a door to fly open. I told myself I'd run at the thugs this time and tackle them. WRAL Reporter Snags Would-Be Thieves! But then I remembered the bloody rag. WRAL Reporter Stabbed Attempting to Foil Robbery!

How I wish I'd caught them or paid more attention, but it had happened so fast, and what did it matter now? But somehow it did matter. In some mixed-up way it did.

I shrugged off the no-good brutes. Stooges! I clenched my fists, peered at the lens, and sucked in a long deep breath. And nailed the standup on the fifth try.

Believe it not, we move pretty fast in our Tar Heel travels, jumping from one story to the next. But fast does not mean fast food. Oh, we love a great old local lunch spot, and there's one of those here in Clayton.

BELIEVE IT NOT, WE MOVE PRETTY FAST IN OUR TAR HEEL TRAVELS, JUMPING FROM ONE STORY TO THE NEXT. BUT FAST DOES NOT MEAN FAST FOOD. OH, WE LOVE A GREAT OLD LOCAL LUNCH SPOT, AND THERE'S ONE OF THOSE HERE IN CLAYTON.

The timing worked beautifully. I pulled open the front door to Jones and stepped inside just as I delivered the last line.

When I poked my head back out, Robert pumped his arm in a *Finally!* gesture. He told me to go ahead in; he was going to grab some extra shots outside. But I think maybe he just needed more air. His face looked a little purple.

I ambled through the restaurant and over to Curtis to thank him. He aimed his spatula at me. "Not so fast," he said and a moment later handed me a basket with two dogs snuggled in waxed paper.

I sat by a pole and set my pad down on the checkered tablecloth. *Aah, yes*, I thought, *a delicious reward at the end of a story.* I even closed my eyes. People probably thought I was praying, but sighing was more like it. Crafting a story is tiring work, though the

real work lay ahead. At some point I'd have to weed through a tangled mishmash of video and sound, extract highlights, string together interviews, and add my narration so that it all flowed and made sense. I was exhausted thinking about it.

I didn't want to think about it, and so I snuggled against the pole and breathed in the warm, spicy scent of Jones Lunch. It smelled like . . . pepperoni pizza. I snapped my eyes open. *Must be the franks and mustard,* I thought and picked up one of the dogs and closed my lids again. And here came those three burly thugs racing through my head. *Jeez.* It was all so jumbled, the robbery intruding on my story. I pictured the bloody rag for the umpteenth time. Well, at least I didn't order ketchup.

I tapped my fingers against the soft tablecloth, glanced around at all the colorful clutter, and listened to the chatter. It seemed important to take it all in. I'd missed one opportunity in Clayton and didn't want another to slip by.

I shot a look out the window even as I picked up the dog, but just a quick look, that's all. The dog had my attention now, and I devoured half of it in one bite, plump and meaty with extra mustard, just the way I liked it. *Yeah, boy!*

I savored the flavor and basked in the moment and warmth of Jones Lunch and felt perfectly content. Safe and secure.

I believe in a TV God but not one draped in a white robe. I see him instead with bulging eyes behind huge horned-rimmed glasses, peering down from a faded billboard. He's advertising for an out-of-practice optometrist.

It's Dr. T. J. Eckleburg from *The Great Gatsby*. The billboard is a symbol in the book and its movie versions. The all-knowing eyes see everything, and the image has stuck with me. In fact, I'd think of Eckleburg whenever fate intervened on my behalf—and fate has repeatedly intervened, so much that I'm sure it's Eckleburg or someone like him who has eyeballed my career path.

In 1984 I was a twenty-two-year-old just out of college. One day I drove to Chattanooga, Tennessee, where I'd lined up two job interviews. "Forget it," the first news director told me. "This market's too big for you. You need experience. Start small." I was so dejected I almost skipped my appointment at the second TV station in town.

But I liked the news director at the next station. He was trying hard to take an interest in me, though I couldn't help notice him fidget while he watched my résumé tape. I'd made the tape when I was an intern at the CBS affiliate in Richmond, Virginia, which I figured would impress him. But when the last story ended, he muttered something about being pleased to meet me, good luck with the search, we'll keep you in mind. He was halfway out of his chair when spur of the moment I said, "I do have this other tape," and pulled it from my briefcase. He hesitated in that halfway position: halfway up, halfway down, frozen in midair. Was he going to stand and show me out or sit and take a look? My future hung in the balance, a foot over the seat cushion.

Dr. T. J. Eckleburg might be a big pair of eyes, but I swear that bespectacled TV God put his hands on the news director's shoulders and shoved him back down.

I had made the other tape in college at Washington and Lee University in Lexington, Virginia, and it contained only one story, seven minutes long, about a string of stores in town that were closing. My teacher wanted to know why. "Find out," he said.

I thought of the assignment as a *60 Minutes* exposé and did my best Morley Safer imitation as the story opened. I strolled down the sidewalk, lowered my voice, confronted the camera, and gestured to a boarded-up storefront.

The news director in Chattanooga, now firmly planted in his chair, leaned close to the TV, and I watched him watching me. He must have seen something because he viewed all seven minutes of my *60 Minutes* special, and news directors almost never watch an entire résumé tape.

Two weeks later he called and offered me the job, and when I hung up the phone I leaped from my chair and did jumping jacks in the living room, and even the tiny salary he'd quoted didn't yank the rug out from under me.

I started at $9,000 a year and rented a furnished one-room apartment with a single window that faced an alley. I woke up each morning to a brick wall. And I loved the place. I was thrilled to be living in Chattanooga and learning the television news business.

But TV news is a *suitcase* business, and after one year in Chattanooga I felt ready to pack my bags for a bigger market. I set up an interview in Winston-Salem, but the interview began as a dud. The beefy, bearded news director was unusually quiet, and we quickly ran out of conversation. That's when he excused himself to check on my résumé tape, which was dubbing in a back edit room. He stayed gone long enough for me to compose my next cover letter in my head; I'd already scratched this job prospect off the list. But when he finally bounded in, he smiled and tossed the tape from one hand to the other like a baseball. He told me he'd entered the edit room just as the last story started to play. It was a quirky feature I'd done in Chattanooga that poked fun at a fancy debutante ball and rowdy beer bash held on the same night. "Great story," he said, grinning and tossing.

Was it coincidence the story began the moment he wandered back to check on the tape? What if he'd excused himself a moment earlier or later? It was the tape's last story—again, news directors almost never watch an entire tape. Any other time he probably wouldn't have bothered to see the piece that won me the job. But then, Dr. T. J. Eckleburg sees everything.

I'd been working in Winston-Salem two years when I met two old moonshiners with two teeth between them at a local fair. Virgil and Lewis were concocting batches of 'shine in a dented copper contraption that looked like a leaning chimney. It was *legal* moonshine. They'd finagled a permit that allowed them to demonstrate how to make it—but not to drink it. Virgil and Lewis winked and grinned, although I winced when they climbed up to dump in another batch. It wasn't the ladder that was so unsteady. It was Virgil and Lewis.

I was looking to climb higher, too, once again to a larger television market, and had sent my moonshiner story to a headhunter agency. The agency copied it onto a big reel with other reporters' stories and shipped the reel to news directors across the country. A news director in Dayton, Ohio, landed on Virgil and Lewis and left a message on my answering machine. "Call me," he said. "We might be interested. You under contract?" In fact, my contract was due to expire the very next day. Virgil and Lewis and their two teeth won me the job. And I think Eckleburg's eyes may have had something to do with it, too.

It was 1990, and I'd been in Dayton for a couple of years when the news director ordered me to his office one night and glared at me through his glasses—which, come to think of it, were also thick horn-rims. He frowned and shook his head. "Convenient interview," he said.

The convenient interview he was talking about involved a woman we both knew. She managed a piece of property for the station, and that particular day I had reported on an issue that affected this woman—probably something to do with zoning laws or property taxes—but the news director saw it instead as an easy "get."

That was the beginning of the end. A short time later he frowned and shook his head again and said he'd give me a few weeks to look for another job. I should have felt devastated. I liked Ohio—and especially the girl I'd met on a blind date in Columbus. We'd had several dates since, and I was full of confidence.

"Know anyone looking to hire? In a bigger market?" I asked. My boldness surprised him and me both, I think. His eyebrows flicked above his horn-rims.

"Well," he said at last, "don't think I'd try for a bigger market. Don't think you'll make it."

I'm sure I surprised him when I did land a bigger job. An overworked news manager with an understaffed newsroom in Raleigh, North Carolina, turned his puffy eyes to the mountain of résumé tapes on the floor beside his desk one day. He sighed and dug his hand deep into the pile.

You'll never guess whose tape he pulled out. Or who might have been peering over his shoulder. Dr. T.J. Eckleburg, I believe.

THE ROAST GRILL

SO MY NEXT HOT DOG STORY WAS NOT DIRECTLY BEHIND WRAL, like Cloos' Coney Island, but it *was* two miles down the road. *Far enough,* I thought. *Not technically a "convenient interview."* That's what I told myself anyway, though realistically I suppose it was truth I was shoving into the distance.

We were on a roll with these hot dog stories; I'd found a recipe the public loved. But right after I'd scheduled our next stop, the news director pulled me aside. "Ease up on the hot dog stories," he said. "Going a little overboard." I explained we were due to shoot another one the next day. He frowned—why do news directors always frown? "Okay," he said. "But make that your last one for a while."

The Roast Grill sat on a side road off Hillsborough Street. About the only reason you'd turn onto that section of West Street would be to eat some HOT WEINERS. The catchy sign hung outside a pale-green building with scraggly vines crawling toward the upstairs window.

The restaurant was tiny: a counter with stools and a few small tables scrunched against the wall. Every seat was taken, and the last thing the place needed was a bulky camera and two news schmucks getting in the way.

"Come on in!" the man at the grill said, pointing a long fork at us with a black hot dog impaled at the end. "Black burned!" he cried and squeezed a bun around the dog and pried it off the prongs. *A burned hot dog?* I thought. "Black burned, medium burned, light burn, no burn," he said—or rather sang—to no one in particular. He was a short, stocky man with a bushy mustache, quick with his hands and light on his feet in that cramped corner of a cooking space. "Seven all the way!" he belted and stabbed and squeezed.

He introduced himself as Hot Dog George, and I grinned, knowing I'd enjoy announcing his name many times in my story. "You can't overdo it," Hot Dog George said, impaling another crispy one, black as coal.

I asked if we could have a few minutes for an interview. "Sure," he said and turned from the grill without signaling somebody else to take over. "Rule one is we keep it simple," he told me on camera and pointed his fork at a picture high on the wall where a white-haired woman with dark eyebrows smiled and held out her arms, displaying two hot dogs in one hand and offering a bottle of Coke with the other. "Grandma, she made the rules. Rule number two is don't change the rules."

Hot Dog George told me his grandparents had come from Greece. "Ellis Island in the '20s," he said, and it occurred to me as he talked that the Roast Grill was its own little island, a landmark on a lonely street, roasting dogs since 1940—burning them, too. The sizzling in the corner grew louder, and I cut off the interview so Hot Dog George and his fork could get back to work.

"He knows when you walk in the door exactly how you want them." The voice sounded familiar, and I turned and saw Cindy sitting at the counter in a bright yellow blouse and stylish straw hat. "Hi, Scotty," she said. I knew Cindy through her parents, who were my neighbors and were like grandparents to my children.

"What are you doing here?" I said. "How are your folks?"

I learned Cindy was a Roast Grill regular and so was her son, Lance, whenever he came home from college. He was home now, elbows on the counter next to her. "His birthday," Cindy said. "Had to celebrate at our favorite place." Lance nodded and grinned. "He has a lot of Roast Grill hot dogs in his twenty-year-old body," she said and nudged him in the ribs.

"Six to go, chili only!" Hot Dog George called. Most people seemed to be ordering the crispy kind, the blacker the better, not a speck of red—none on top of the dog, either. Hot Dog George pointed his fork at an odd sign shaped like a ketchup bottle with a bold *X* marked across it. "Ketchup just really doesn't belong on a good hot dog," said Hot Dog George. *Good thing he hasn't outlawed mustard*, I thought.

I looked around at all the colorful knickknacks and laughed at the battery-operated dancing Coke bottle that bent and jiggled on the shelf next to Grandma's picture. But I still worried about being in the way, so I slid off to a corner where I discovered yellowed newspaper clippings taped to the wall. A man at a table waved his burned hot dog at the IN MEMORIAM sign above, and I realized the clippings were obituaries. He told me he'd known many of the faces peering from the print. "Frank, he used to come in every day."

I studied the faces and read about their lives and wondered how many years they'd visited the Roast Grill, how many birthdays they'd spent with friends at the counter and "black-burned" on the plate. *Black burned,* I wrote on my pad and next to it, *ashes to ashes.* I grinned at the play on words. But no, the sentiment didn't feel right, and I scratched it out.

The faces seemed important somehow, and I stepped back and searched my mind, and before I knew it I was looking into the sweet tired eyes of Grandma with her outstretched arms. I wondered how difficult that must have been leaving Greece, landing at Ellis Island, starting from scratch in a foreign land. I pondered what Grandma's picture did not show, the hard work and sacrifice, and I turned to the In Memoriam wall again and read the names and studied the grainy faces and the words came:

> A MAN AT A TABLE WAVED HIS BURNED HOT DOG AT THE "IN MEMORIAM" SIGN ABOVE, AND I REALIZED THE CLIPPINGS WERE OBITUARIES. HE TOLD ME HE'D KNOWN MANY OF THE FACES PEERING FROM THE PRINT. "FRANK, HE USED TO COME IN EVERY DAY."

If the walls could talk, they'd talk of the dogs and days at Roast Grill. And the dreams of the Roast Grill.

I looked up to see Hot Dog George standing beside me—oh, no, he'd abandoned the grill again. "One of the big things Grandma left me with was try and keep this place making hot dogs," he said and fell silent, and even the sizzling seemed to settle into a dull hiss.

But the silence abruptly shattered, like a ketchup bottle that explodes when an opera singer reaches the piercing apex of a screeching note. Indeed, an opera singer was in the house: George's sister who worked the grill when not on stage. "Happy birthday to yooouuu!" she belted to twenty-year-old Lance. "Happy birthday to yooouuu!"

I smiled and thought of Lance's grandparents, my neighbors, and wished they were here. They were nearing eighty, but what a thrill it would have been, no matter the tight squeeze and ear-splitting note. I thought of *their* love for their family and how they'd embraced my own children.

Men at the counter reached around and patted Lance on the shoulder, and Cindy glowed—and not just because of her bright yellow blouse. She and Lance were among strangers who didn't seem like strangers but friends, and it seemed they were all part of something special. Even the faces on the wall were part of it, if only in spirit.

"Happy birthday to yooo—uu—uuu."

I reached for my pad again:

If these walls could talk they just might sing.

JOHNSON'S HAMBURGERS

FAIRNESS RULES—IN JOURNALISM AND IN TASTE BUDS. I WAS doing all these hot dog stories and leaving the poor hamburger out to dry. But then I remembered meeting a man years ago named Mr. Johnson and how proud he was of his Siler City restaurant, even taking me outside to the back and leaning halfway into the dumpster. *Whoa,* I thought, trying not to breathe in through my nose. He grunted and reached and pulled out a flattened cardboard box and pointed to the label. "Right there, right there," he said. "USDA prime. Best quality meat you can buy. That's the secret, and we buy it fresh every day."

He hustled me inside and grabbed a block of Velveeta as big as a brick. "Right there, right there," he said, jabbing a finger at the *V* on the wrapper. He peeled it open, sliced a hunk, and stamped it on a sizzling burger, and man, oh man, did I ever breathe through my nose then. I sucked in the cheesy scent and felt my mouth water.

I hadn't heard of Johnson's Hamburgers when I arrived at WRAL in 1997, and people in the newsroom didn't bring it up either when one day I mentioned I was headed to Siler City. What they said instead was, "You gonna visit Aunt Bee?"

"Aunt Bee?"

"Yeah. You know she's buried in Siler City? Bring some pickles with you."

"Pickles?" I'd recently moved from Virginia and felt suddenly out of place now that I was south of the state line. *Pickles? What do pickles have to do with Siler City?*

At least I didn't have to ask about Aunt Bee. Even growing up in Massachusetts I used to watch the *Andy Griffith Show* and laugh at the innocent shenanigans in the fictional southern town of Mayberry. The real-life town of Siler City was actually mentioned in the show, and the actress who played Aunt Bee apparently thought it sounded like a nice, quiet community. The actress, Frances Bavier, retired to Siler City in 1972, once telling a reporter, "I fell in love with North Carolina, all the pretty roads and trees."

Bavier died at her Siler City home in 1989. She left $100,000 to the local police department and her house to the hospital. Today it's not unusual to see jars of pickles resting on her tombstone in Oakwood Cemetery. The jars are a tribute to an episode in which Aunt Bee enters her homemade pickles in the county fair.

I was looking forward to the trip shortly after landing the job at WRAL. The pickles had piqued my curiosity, along with a newspaper article that described Siler City as a quaint town of front porches and churches. I only wished my assignment was a little more folksy.

WRAL had hired me to produce documentaries, and I was working on a piece about immigration. Siler City was grappling with a major influx of Hispanics, drawn to jobs at the chicken-processing plants.

When the photographer and I drove into town, I did see quite a few front porches and churches, but as we began shooting interviews I quickly realized this wasn't the Mayberry I knew—although it may have been for the immigrants. A translator helped me decipher the dreams of the Spanish-speaking newcomers, and I noticed their eyes grow wide the faster they talked, faces glowing with the promise of a better life. I enjoyed their enthusiasm but at the same time wondered about all the old-timers in Siler City and whether *their* eyes had opened wide.

IT WAS JUST HOW A CLASSIC HAMBURGER JOINT SHOULD BE: FULL OF CLATTER AND CHATTER, MEN LAUGHING, LADIES SMILING AND SWAPPING GOSSIP, CASH REGISTER CLANKING, WAITRESSES HOLLERING.

I needed a place to sample local opinion and peered out the window while puttering through town, and that's when I spotted the big red-and-white sign by the side of the road: Johnson's Hamburgers Since 1946. We pulled in and parked.

It was just how a classic hamburger joint should be: full of clatter and chatter, men laughing, ladies smiling and swapping gossip, cash register clanking, waitresses hollering. "Need another cheeseburger!" There were plenty of booths, but the counter seemed like the place to be. It stretched from the grill at one end to the wall at the other. Men in work boots and ball caps and button-downs and ties swiveled on green-padded seats propped on poles and watched the short-order action.

The cheese! Those huge yellowy-orange hunks melting over the burgers and oozing onto the angry grill. And the smell! That greasy, meaty, cheesy, delectable smell. I'm not sure Aunt Bee would have approved—I can't picture her eating anything with her hands—but I think ol' Andy would have jumped right in. And I bet he would have enjoyed shooting the breeze with Mr. Johnson.

Claxton Johnson was like a character straight out of Mayberry, down-home and friendly. He was built like Gomer on the *Andy Griffith Show,* tall and thin. And like Goober at the gas station in Mayberry, he wasn't afraid to get his hands greasy, rolling hamburger meat in his palms so that the burgers came out round as ball bearings. He plopped them on the grill in neat rows and went down the line with his spatula, mashing each one like they were accelerator pedals.

It was only after he'd fed me one of his cheeseburger sensations—*Oh, my gosh, the Velveeta!*—that I began to get hold of myself and put on my news face and ask about all the new faces in town. Mr. Johnson was busy at the grill, so I posed my immigration questions to people at the counter. It was uncanny how many picked that time to take huge bites and gesture that they couldn't talk.

I couldn't blame them. It was a touchy topic, and I felt bad for bringing it up. I suppose even then the feature-reporter side of me was warring with the newshound side—and to be honest, I was glad the feature side won out.

I did not get the explosive interviews I was looking for that day, but I did meet some mighty nice folks and enjoyed a delicious meal. Johnson's was like Mayberry, where life is simple and everybody's happy, and I hoped all of Siler City was the same, even though I knew I'd have to search for my sound bites someplace else in town. But at the moment, I felt satisfied—my belly did, too—and I was content to leave the Mayberry image intact.

———

Reporters are all about uncovering the truth. Small towns are all about quaintness and charm—I always picture white picket fences. But which side of the fence is reality really on? A fine line can separate truth from myth.

I left the Mayberry image intact for ten years, often thinking of Johnson's whenever I'd bite into a burger somewhere. *Pretty good*, I'd think. *But nothing like the one I had that day in Siler City.*

Even while I was sampling all those hot dogs on my Tar Heel Traveler jaunts, Johnson's was never far from my mind. What a classic it was, and to some extent the place became my standard to which I compared every other place. My hot dog segments were popular, but I began to think maybe it was time to throw some hamburger stories into the mix—and return to Mayberry.

Times had changed in ten years. I had access to the Internet now, and before setting out, I punched the words *Johnson's Hamburgers* into my computer and found it was still going strong, still serving Velveeta cheeseburgers. I rubbed my hands together and felt water already collecting under my tongue. But then I remembered that old documentary and for grins typed in *Siler City*.

Holy cow! I read that Spanish-speaking residents comprised half the town's population now. The chicken plants seemed to be doing well. Schools had hired more teachers, police had hired more officers, and the town had generated more tax money. And people were still leaving pickles on Aunt Bee's tombstone.

I smiled as I read, the way people do when they watch a funny TV show. But my smile shrank the more I read, and I'm sure my brow wrinkled so that my face must have looked as haggard as that of Otis, the Mayberry town drunk, when he's dying for a drink. The woman who played Aunt Bee, I learned, was no Aunt Bee. As the newspaper put it, "She Fell for the Mayberry Myth."

According to the paper, Bavier admitted she'd made a mistake moving to Siler City. She said fans of the show irked her; they pestered her and peeked in her windows. She became a recluse, living alone in her twenty-room house, just she and her fourteen cats. Andy Griffith and Ron Howard stopped by one day unannounced, two fellow actors she'd shared so much success with on the show, but Bavier refused to let them in. Neither one attended her funeral.

After she died people who entered her house said it smelled awful. Her fourteen cats had used the basement shower as a litter box. Newspaper accounts described dark rooms with worn upholstery, frayed carpets, and peeling plaster. Her only mementos from the show were a few hats and dresses. The big find was a 1966 Studebaker. The green two-door sedan sat slumped in the garage with four flat tires and a dented fender.

And then there were the pickles on the TV show. The pickles were horrible.

I read about the episode I'd apparently missed. Aunt Bee tries to outdo her friend Clara, whose homemade pickles have won eleven blue ribbons at the county fair. But Clara's pickles are good, while Aunt Bee's taste like they've been floating in kerosene. She'll be a laughingstock if she enters them in the fair, so Andy and sidekick Barney hatch a plan. Except it backfires, and in the end they're forced to eat eight awful quarts of the kerosene cucumbers.

I wondered if placing pickles on Bavier's tombstone was some kind of cryptic insult. One article said she despised the Aunt Bee role and that during filming everybody around her walked on eggshells. And yet her headstone is inscribed AUNT BEE and TO LIVE IN THE HEARTS OF THOSE LEFT BEHIND IS NOT TO DIE.

I pushed away from my desk, feeling more like Otis than ever, Otis with a hangover, still a little drunk with the sweetness of Mayberry but shaken by the bitterness of truth. Mayberry seemed suddenly complicated. And I feared Siler City was, too.

Mr. Johnson hadn't changed a bit in ten years. And neither had the cheeseburgers. He cut a hunk of Velveeta, punched it on a sizzling patty, clapped me on the shoulder, and asked if I was ready. "One burger or two?" Then he cocked a gray eyebrow. "Or three?"

I swallowed the tingle in my taste buds before holding up my notepad. "Not yet," I said. I had interviews to do and sentences to scribble, and one came to me right then: *Talk about burgers—call these the big cheese!*

"He puts a hunk on them, he really does," said a man at the counter with a napkin balled in one hand and a half-eaten burger in the other.

Johnson's was the same as it was before, and I mean exactly the same, as if the restaurant had been locked in a freezer with tomorrow's supply of meat. Brown was still the dominant color—brown walls, counter, booths, and of course the burgers. Mr. Johnson flattened them with his spatula and accented them with that luscious cheese, and another line of script oozed from my pen:

You'd think time would have a way of squashing a little place like this, but Johnson's is still cookin'.

"We've been here since 1946," said Mr. Johnson's daughter, an energetic redhead who worked behind the grill. "My grandparents opened it," she said and showed me a photograph of her grandparents and one of her dad as a kid. Mr. Johnson peered at himself over her shoulder.

"Yeah, I was a little boy out there catching curb," he said.

"Catching curb?" I asked.

He told me his folks used to offer curb service. People would pull up and order from the boy at their window who'd run in and dash out with a tray full of hot food and cold drinks. He didn't get around on roller skates but he did have to dress nice. Young Claxton Johnson wore a button-down shirt and khaki pants. The older Claxton Johnson studied the picture and smiled.

There was no curb service anymore, so that was one change at Johnson's. And I couldn't help but wonder about other changes, too—the ones beyond the walls.

I raised the issue ever so gently. "Chicken plants doing well? How about the workers who came from Mexico? They getting along okay in town?"

Most people shrugged and said, "Pretty good. Just fine."

The food is what most people wanted to talk about. "I tell you, I believe it's the best meat you can buy," one man told me. When I asked about the Hispanic folks he said they were the best, too. "Hard workers."

A moment later, Mr. Johnson rapped his knuckles on the counter. "Sittdown, sittdown," he said. I did and he set a burger in front of me. I was tempted to peel off the bun for a look-see, but it was obvious the Velveeta had done its work. Cheese dripped down the sides and mingled with the meaty juices.

"Haven't you heard?" asked Mr. Johnson's daughter who threw me an adorable grin. "It's the best cheeseburgers you'll ever get."

I grabbed it with both hands and opened wide, grinning with anticipation, certain it would taste just like I remembered—and nothing at all like Aunt Bee's pickles. I stifled a laugh and took the biggest bite I could.

How to describe it other than "Oh, my gosh!"

I'm sure Andy would have said, "Don't that beat all."

Aunt Bee might have sighed good-naturedly. "Oh, Andy."

And Frances Bavier? "No. Thank. You!"

I shook hands with Mr. Johnson, told him it was great seeing him again and stumbled for the door, like Otis after a few too many. All that scrumptious flavor must have rushed to my head, not to mention my belly. I was plenty good and full.

I stepped outside into the bustling world of Siler City. Johnson's Hamburgers was on the main thoroughfare, and traffic rumbled by, except when the light turned red. Trucks shuddered, squealed, and hissed, before growling into gear again and thundering on. *Probably headed to a chicken plant*, I thought, remembering those glowing faces from long ago, and it then occurred to me I had not seen one of those faces inside Johnson's. I suppose some borders are harder to cross, and I wasn't sure how I felt about that. I wasn't even sure how I felt about myself. I thought I'd buried my cynicism, traded in my old news face when I'd transformed into the Tar Heel Traveler. But some things never change.

Johnson's was the same as ever, and so was Mayberry—or at least that's what I wanted to believe. And people were still leaving pickles on Aunt Bee's tombstone, though I sure hoped they didn't taste like kerosene. I hoped the pickles were the best pickles you could buy, nice and sweet, just like Aunt Bee herself. I wanted to believe that, too.

Before leaving Johnson's that day, a couple people elbowed me and said, "Where you heading next, the stockyards?" They grinned and I laughed. It was a joke, right? Burgers, meat, cows, stockyards. I even elbowed them back before turning away and thinking, *Huh?*

I didn't give it much thought after that, not until e-mails started trickling in after our story on Johnson's aired. The e-mails went something like this:

Yeah, Johnson's is good all right, but check out the stockyards. They got the cattle auction every Monday and Friday. And the restaurant, too. Burgers out of this world! This place is one of a kind.

I was sure it was no joke a short time later when I spotted a magazine spread about Carolina Stockyards near Siler City. The article, the e-mails, and the coincidental timing of the two were like lassos tugging me back to Chatham County, and I didn't resist. Truth is, I was curious about a restaurant at a stockyard. Sounded like the punch line to a good story.

I grew up a city boy near Boston, but I do love playing the cowboy. When I arrived I hooked my thumbs to my belt buckle and waddled bowlegged across the gravel lot, purposely kicking up dust with the cowboy boots I'd retrieved from my attic. Years ago on a trip to Texas I'd forked out a bundle of money to buy a pair, which seemed like a good idea at the time. But when I got back to Raleigh and went clodhopping around the grocery store on my first test run, I had the feeling people were inspecting *me* instead of the produce. I rarely wore the boots again.

The stockyard owner gripped my hand and slapped my back and hurried me around the side of the building, eager to show off his top-quality cattle. We rounded the corner where dozens of cows stood and swayed and stomped in a large pen. The owner talked on and on, shouting over the mooing, and didn't seem the least bit embarrassed when one cow after another lifted its tail and relieved itself. "Bet you must be hungry," he said after a while. "We got the best patties around."

He gestured to the building, which was long, wide, and flat, and told me to make myself at home. I pushed open the double glass doors and stood in a lobby with wooden doors on either side and signs above them. I faced a choice: turn right for the auction or left for the restaurant. I chose right because the owner had been wrong. I wasn't hungry, not with the smell of cow patties still in my nose.

I stepped into a big bowl of a room with auditorium seating that looked down on a center ring. A cowboy was struggling with a rope looped around a black bull and the bull wasn't budging. Three other cowpokes scurried up behind, planted their hands on the animal's rump and shoved, as though pushing a Hummer with a dead battery. They finally corralled the bull and rammed the latch.

A platform rose above the ring and a man at a microphone prattled almost poetically in a sing-song voice, which made me think of my favorite poet, Robert Service, and his rollicking ballads. The beat sounded the same, except the auctioneer spoke ten times too fast. *Got . . . seventy-five . . . one on four . . . sold!* But the rugged men in their seats must have understood because their eyes zeroed right in on the ring, and every few seconds one of them would nod their head or raise a finger or twitch their hand, which affected the auctioneer's rhythm. His voice rose, leveled off, then peaked again.

I'd seen auctions before of course; in fact, every year Nina and I attend the Raleigh Roundup, a cancer fund-raiser with a western theme. Oh, I do love playing the cowboy. The event is the one time my lonely boots see the light of day. I also pull on faded jeans and a plaid shirt and top off my duds with a red-checked bandana strung around my neck—though Nina tells me to yank the silly thing off before walking inside.

The Raleigh Roundup includes a real auctioneer with high-priced paintings and weekend getaways up for grabs, but people mill around sipping cocktails during the action, and nods and hand twitches wouldn't stand a chance. Bidders must bounce on their toes, wave their hands, and shout to be heard.

I wanted to be as inconspicuous as possible at the stockyard auction. I worried about moving a muscle and inadvertently buying a heifer. "Sold!" crowed the auctioneer and paused a half minute while another bull entered the ring, and in that time I shuttled to the back of the room, froze against the wall, waited for another "Sold!" and then crouched and tapped the man in the seat in front of me.

"I'm with a TV station," I muttered. "Can I interview you?" You'd think I would have surprised him, but the man's lazy gray eyes didn't bob a bit. I suppose he saw me as just another skittish calf that had wandered from home. He nodded almost imperceptibly, probably out of pity. "Whaddaya think of the auction?" I asked.

"Good cows," he said, which is all he had time to say. The auctioneer called for the next bull. But the bull wouldn't come out of the pen and two cowboys had to climb in and wrestle it out, which got me thinking. *That's what I need to do. Grab the bull by the horns.*

Between bidding, I circled the auditorium till I came to a door at the base of the platform. I figured it would be locked, but it wasn't. I pushed it open and took the stairs and next thing I knew stood directly behind the man at the microphone. If I'd worn my red-checked bandana I would've been tempted to slip it over my mouth bank-robber-style, like Dangerous Dan McGrew in Robert Service's well-known ballad. The auctioneer was obviously busy, so I targeted the man to his right whose face glowed in the reflected light of a computer screen. I waited for another break in the bidding before making my move.

The computer man's eyes did bob, though I don't think he was surprised by the interruption but dizzy from staring at his screen instead. I was surprised by the size of the neon numbers. Most began with a two, followed by a comma. He said the bidders were mainly from large farms in states out west, which in my mind upped the ante. I began to realize how much money those little hand twitches and head nods meant. It was mesmerizing watching it all from up high, detecting the idiosyncrasies of the auction. But I didn't have all day. I still had half a story and more beef to wrangle—the kind that didn't moo but sizzled.

I retraced my steps, slipped out of the auditorium, ducked into the lobby again and crossed to the door on the other side. I opened it and stepped into a vast hall that led to the Carolina Restaurant. People waiting to enter the restaurant saw the camera and waved with a "By all means, jump in, cut the line, come on." They were nice folks, and I thanked them and squeezed past.

The restaurant was full and nothing fancy, which was part of its appeal. The tables weren't arranged in any particular order, just scattered about and topped with the usual condiment bottles. People ate off paper plates and chowed on burgers and dogs. I watched the cook cut hunks of Velveeta and thought, *Déjà vu. Must be something about cheese and Siler City.*

"Do people come here for the cattle auction or the food?" I shouted over the grill.

"Both!" the cook shouted back and laughed. "But the food sure is good!"

I turned to the tables and introduced myself to an old-timer with the craggy look of a longtime cattle hand. His white mustache looped down at the corners of his mouth. "Is it strange having a restaurant next to a stock-yard?" I asked.

He shrugged. "Not really. You know farmers; we got to eat, too."

I was surprised at the number of moms and children and envied a curly-headed girl who hadn't been afraid to wear *her* bandana, a bright pink one nicely ruffled around her neck. She chomped a burger, and what a beautiful shot that was. "Monday and Friday are the days to go to the stockyard and have a hamburger," said her mom. "And make sure you keep your hands down while you're in the auction. Don't wiggle, don't touch your ears or anything." I knew what she meant.

I interviewed many other folks and before leaving sampled a cheese-burger myself, which was delicious—so long as I didn't think about the cattle across the lobby.

I thanked everybody and walked through the hall and out the door and into the building's lobby and stood a moment between doors, the restaurant on one side, auditorium on the other. I could hear the auctioneer's chant through the wall and considered poking my head back in, but I had so much sound recorded on camera already that I was overwhelmed. All his auction-eering and the interviews I'd gathered—I'd have to weed through reams of tape back at the station and somehow tie two halves into one story. They were like separate stories. *How to put two and two together?* I was whooped thinking about it, felt the walls closing in, and needed to breathe; I pushed open the double glass doors that led outside.

I kicked up dust on the way to the car but only because I dragged my feet. I knew I had a story packed with potential but at the same time felt trampled by an audio/video stampede. And I'd done it to myself, let the herd run wild. And then came another kick to the head.

"Channel 5!" boomed a voice that jolted me, and I glanced up to see a slender man with salt-and-pepper hair hustling my way. "The Tar Heel Traveler!" he cried. *A fan*, I thought, but when he pumped my hand, he said he knew my boss, Jim Goodmon, CEO of Capitol Broadcasting, parent com-pany of WRAL. The ante had suddenly skyrocketed, and I told myself, *Hold on, get a grip, focus.*

"You doing a story on the stockyard?" he asked. "When's it gonna be on? This week? Next week?" I said I didn't know yet. "Can I get a copy of it, a DVD? Be glad to pay you." I told him a production company did that for us and charged a fee. His smile shriveled. "Oh, well," he sighed. "Guess I'll just have to keep an eye out. I'll be sure to tell Jim I saw you," he said and turned for the building.

I'd been thrown for a loop and my chin thumped to my chest. I was whooped, all right, my story and quite possibly my reputation in tatters. My eyes fell on my ridiculous pointy-toed boots that looked like dried snakeskin. I kicked the gravel and a rock the size of my belt buckle catapulted into the air as if from a slingshot and crashed to the ground fifty feet away. *Whoa*, I thought and took a second look at the boots. Maybe it wasn't snakeskin they resembled but rawhide, tough and rugged. The feisty spirit of Dangerous Dan McGrew began to rumble through my bones.

I suppose life is a choice: door number one or door number two. You can sit by and observe or take a stand. And raise a hand. I raised mine, raised it and waved it and bounced on my pointy toes and shouted, "Sir! Wait just a minute!"

My boss's friend stopped midstride, and I ran to him like a duck, but, shoot, it was hard enough *walking* in cowboy boots. I asked if I could interview him even as I thought, *Am I a glutton for punishment or what? Another interview? But shoot, what's one more?*

"Well, I think it's fantastic," he said on camera, meaning both the auction and the restaurant. "We're losing this kind of thing, and we shouldn't. It gets you back to your roots, and roots are important. We can't forget our roots, no sir."

He made several other articulate comments and after the interview I pumped *his* hand. His remarks had put the whole piece in perspective, had helped tie together all those loose ends, and that's what I'd been missing, that focus. I could hardly wait to tell Mr. Goodmon I'd seen his buddy at the stockyard.

I turned and hooked my thumbs to my belt and breathed in deep—and coughed when I caught a whiff of cattle. But I smiled anyway and walked bow-legged to the car, kicking stones along the way. I even let out a whoop. "Yee-haw!" I cried to no one in particular. Oh yeah, I do love playing the cowboy.

ODE TO BARBECUE

WRITING THIS CHAPTER IS TOUGH. IT'S A NO-WIN SITUATION. There's eastern-style barbecue and western style, and if I profile a particular barbecue joint I'm forced to choose a side, and the other side will no doubt accuse me of bias, inaccuracy, stupidity, and of generally having no idea what I'm talking about.

Barbecue is a far different animal than hot dogs and hamburgers. North Carolinians are passionate about them, too, but barbecue cuts to the bone, to the state's red-clay core, you might say.

I was born in North Carolina but raised in Massachusetts, and you'd think I'd love lobster and barbecue both, but I'm not real big on either. I don't mind barbecue, both western and eastern, but I'll take a juicy burger with a hunk of Velveeta or two crispy dogs with extra mustard over a platter of chopped pork and hush puppies. Maybe the diehards are right. Maybe I really don't have any idea what I'm talking about.

But I do know when to be careful. Barbecue is a battlefield. Folks in western North Carolina tend to cook only the pig's shoulders and serve the meat with a tomato-type sauce. Eastern-style sauce is vinegar based, and the whole hog gets plunked on the grill. The two sides are adamant theirs is the best.

My wife will tell you I don't like conflict, which is why she wins every argument—I think she likes being married to me. I enjoy life unruffled, smooth, and easy with peace and quiet on the home front and in the work-place. Best to stay away from the fray and avoid conflict at all cost. And so as the Tar Heel Traveler, I've been reluctant to dip a tongue into the barbecue civil war. If I were to do a barbecue story west of Raleigh, the folks east of Raleigh might flip the channel or hurl a pig hoof at the TV, and vice versa. But the trouble is, you can't exactly live in North Carolina without stepping

on red clay, and you can't travel the state without confronting a cooked pig. Both are inevitable.

I was planning one of our western trips, eventually aiming for Asheville or Bryson City or someplace closer to Tennessee than Raleigh, but as usual I'd begun to set up several stories along the way. The idea is to shoot as many as you can in the time you have, given the distance traveled. One night in a hotel between two days on the road might yield seven or eight stories. Then we can hunker down at the station for a week or two writing and editing—and taking our wives to dinner.

I pulled my West file, traced our route, and picked out stories that fell along the path. One idea somebody submitted was about a longtime barbecue place in a small town off I-40 west of Raleigh. We'd be driving right by it—though I'll refrain from naming it, and you'll soon understand why.

I stared at the sheet of paper a long time while civil war thundered inside my head.

Lord have mercy, you're crazy, man? roared one side of my brain. *Don't do it. Don't even think it. Those eastern folks'll eat you alive. Oh, you're asking for trouble, mister. Don't be going near any barbecue, not even with a ten-foot fork, you hear? You listening? Dude, I'm serious.*

But the other side of my brain butted in.

Oh, c'mon. It's another story, piece of cake. You'll be in and outta there in an hour tops. And you know they're gonna give you free barbecue. And iced tea. You love iced tea. Whatchya waiting for, my man? Call 'em. It's one more for the stockpile. Oh, yeah, BBQ on the house!

I picked up the phone and dialed the place.

It was a plain white building by the side of the road. The viewer who'd written me insisted it was the best barbecue around, slow-cooked over hot coals, the way it's supposed to be, and the same family had run it for generations. So I didn't worry how small and drab the building looked, didn't give much thought to the stains streaking from the roof. I ignored the grimy sign and greasy front window. In fact, I felt drawn to the place because it did look old and worn. Aren't those hole-in-the-wall dives the best, the ones that look ramshackle outside but brim with character and good eats inside?

Get yourself on in, piped one side of my head. *We got a story to shoot. And vittles to eat!*

I sucked in a breath and opened the door, preparing myself for the attention we usually attract. I'm sure most people think, "What? A TV crew from Raleigh coming to our little town? Oh, boy!" But when we walked through the door people kept eating or staring out the window. We could have been invisible, which was fine by me; there was no reason to be self-conscious. I liked the place already, except the room did seem awfully dim. I don't like eating under bright lights either, but even I was thinking somebody ought to crank the blinds a smidge. Maybe that's why nobody paid attention to our camera—the room was too dark.

Low light, blue-and-white tablecloths, padded seats—the place should have felt warm and cozy, but almost everyone wore their winter jackets while they ate. It was one of those raw March days, although the temperature inside was actually comfortable. Maybe they were in a hurry and had some other place to go. In any case, I figured I'd better interview them quick. All those bulky parkas made me a little jumpy.

It was time to get started, but we'd been standing inside the door for five minutes and the same waitress had crossed in front of us half a dozen times without a hello. When she wasn't handing out menus she was carrying big trays of food, and I didn't blame her for staying focused. She certainly didn't want to stumble. The floor was warped.

I decided it was time to take the initiative, and so I marched toward the swinging door I'd seen the waitress repeatedly bump open with her backside. I used my hand instead.

It opened to a large kitchen with a glowing fire pit off to the side. A tall man was shoveling in coal, triggering an explosion of sparks which sounded like a hundred people snapping their fingers. I told him who we were and asked if we could take some pictures. "Mind throwing in a little more?" I asked. He shrugged, piled another mound onto his shovel, and heaved it in. The snapping sparks made for great video.

"Another five hours to go and we'll be ready to roll," said the coal man. It was lunchtime but he was already cooking for the dinner crowd.

No one told us not to shoot, so we shot. We focused on two ladies spreading dollops of barbecue onto bun after bun, and when the coal man began chopping pork with mini machetes in each hand—*rat-a-tat-tat!*—I was pretty sure I had the opening to my story. Granted, the man was perspiring like a pig, but I figured we could edit out the sweat dripping off his nose.

The kitchen door bumped open, and the waitress appeared rear end first. She set her empty tray on the counter and shoved her hand into a bowl of hush puppies. She grabbed a hunk and threw the puppies onto a plate and grabbed more and did the same.

Wait a minute, I thought. *Isn't that the waitress I saw handing out menus?* I wondered how many random fingers had touched those menus.

She was plunging both hands into the bowl now and slinging hush puppies like popcorn. Several skittered along the counter, but no worries. She scooped them up and plopped them in their rightful place. At least she kept her hands free of the door. She butted it open and was gone.

We exited the kitchen soon after. By then, the sweaty coal man had sealed the pit and was chopping again on the counter; in fact, right where the random hush puppies had fallen a moment before.

I searched the dining room, keeping one eye out for the owner and another for the restaurant rating. I spotted it on the wall: 91. "Don't set foot in a restaurant below 92," our consumer reporter warned me once. A 91 is a B, but in restaurant lingo B stands for Bad.

A woman finally approached, her matching visor and shirt the same color as the tablecloths. She had blonde hair and a nice figure and looked about thirty-five, except for the eyes. Her eyes looked sixty-five. A puffy bag squatted under each one.

She introduced herself and told me her grandfather had started the place in the 1940s. Then her dad ran it, and now she'd taken over. She talked about how proud she was of her family and how her dad would trudge through snowstorms and open the restaurant so that people who lost power would have somewhere to eat. I thought she was going to cry as she told the story, but maybe it was just her puffy eyes. Or maybe she *was* going to cry.

"It's hard," she said. "People would not believe how hard this is." Her body sagged, and she started to lean as if to lay her head on my shoulder. I almost held out my arms to catch her. Or maybe she was leaning because of the warped floor. "I don't know how much longer I can do this," she whimpered, apparently forgetting the camera. We were still rolling, but I doubted I'd use her confession. It would blow the whole feel-good aura of the piece.

I interviewed a few of the regulars. One man made a show of pushing up his jacket sleeves, dipping his sandwich in barbecue sauce and displaying it for the camera. "It's great," he said. "Look at that piece of meat." But I had trouble seeing the meat through the sauce. And nobody had yet bothered to crank the window blinds.

We were on a tight time schedule, but I felt the need to give the place a fair shake. Maybe the meal would dispel my doubts. The chef had told me it took him ten hours to cook a pig. The least I could do was sample his hard work.

The waitress slapped a couple menus on the table and disappeared without a word. Eventually we flagged her down and ordered some barbecue sandwiches. I was hungry but ate slowly, tentatively, like I was eating fish. I kept searching my mouth for bones—or strands of stray hair. I ate with my jacket on and ignored the hush puppies.

When it was time to pay the bill I figured the cashier might wave me through, but she took my ten and told me to come back soon. *Holy mackerel!* both sides of my brain yelped. *Where's the change? Jeez Louise!*

I had another Tar Heel Traveler story to add to the stockpile, but I wondered if it was a story I should tell. "'Course you should," bellowed the photographer. "You got the whole history of the place, the poor guy driving through blizzards to feed folks, three generations running the joint, pig cooked the old way. We got nothing to do with restaurant ratings. Let the people decide if they wanna go." He slapped his palms on the wheel, stepped on the gas and never looked back.

The story aired two weeks later, and soon after I received the following e-mail:

I rode with my wife to have some good ole NC BBQ. The food was Ok. However, this is the filthiest place I have ever been in that served food. I have seen floors in a hog parlor that were cleaner. Thanks.

I chuckled at the hog parlor line. And then I read the next e-mail:

I saw your Tar Heel Traveler *last night and went to this place to eat. We were not pleased at all with the BBQ. Also, did you notice the sanitation grade? 91. The bathroom was dirty around the outside of the commode. The hand dryer would not even come on. I had to use toilet tissue to dry my hands. I'm just wondering how much more there was wrong (in the kitchen) to have this grade. Maybe Monica should visit it. Thanks.*

Monica is the station's consumer reporter, the one who tells folks which restaurants have the highest and lowest ratings. Her reports are popular, in part because of all the sound effects the editor adds: smashing plates, breaking glass, lots of oohs and aahs. Mention cockroaches and it's a cacophony of ugghs.

I let out an uggh of my own when the next message popped in. It was from Monica:

The restaurant you featured recently received its FOURTH "B" grade in a row. Family owned or not, that is NOT good. While a poor sanitation grade is not something you would typically be concerned with in a Tar Heel Traveler *story, we need to at least pay attention to it. WRAL has become known as the "restaurant sanitation leader," and NOT paying attention is kind of like talking out of both sides of our "news mouth." Their BBQ may TASTE good, but they clearly have serious cleanliness problems. Thanks!*

Well, at least Monica and the other letter writers had all ended their notes with *Thanks.* I appreciated the southern hospitality and mulled the feedback. A few other e-mails were positive. *Excellent story,* one man wrote. *They're one of the few places left that serve sliced as well as chopped BBQ. Thanks!*

Monica was probably right. I should have checked the rating right away and moved on to the next story. But then I thought of the chef, slaving in front of that hot pit for ten hours. And the blonde baggy-eyed owner who loved her daddy and was doing what she could to carry on the family legacy. Maybe our story would give them a boost. I pictured her dashing to the bathroom, mop in one hand and fresh rolls of toilet paper in the other. Maybe the waitress would stick to just handing out menus. The ladies in the kitchen could sure use some hairnets. They were all hard-working folks; it's just that they needed more folks to lend a hand—preferably a latex-covered hand.

From now on I told myself I'd check the restaurant rating. *Attaboy!* said one side of my brain. But from now on I wasn't sure I wanted to do any more barbecue stories.

Told you so, piped the other side of my brain.

Least you coulda done was score us a free meal! they cried in unison. *Jeez Louise!*

BILL'S BARBECUE

THERE'S GOOD EATIN' IN WILSON. IT'S ONE OF THOSE LAID-BACK North Carolina towns peppered with down-home restaurants. Spend a day in Wilson and it's easy to find three great meals at three local landmarks. The hard part's deciding which moms-and-pops to visit for breakfast, lunch, and dinner when there are so many to choose from. You can't lose when you're headed east of Raleigh on an empty stomach. Grab the Wilson exit and take your pick.

Wilson is especially known for two barbecue empires whose names tower over the whole hog-eating region. Hunting for some good 'cue? You got Parker's and you got Bill's. Forget breakfast. Save lunch for one, dinner at the other, and you'll be slap happy as a pig.

I was curious about both empires, how they came to be so well known. I'd been to a big neighborhood cookout in Raleigh and found out Bill's had catered it. "Bills? In Wilson?" I asked the host. "But that's an hour away."

"Oh, yeah," she said, a warm barbecue plate in one hand, a frosty Budweiser in the other. "Go get you one," she said, but I may have misunderstood. I headed for the cooler instead of the grill.

Every so often a collection of stories will pop up in one place, and one day at work I found myself with a nice pile of e-mails from Wilson. Folks there had sent me some good ideas, and I was eager to dig in. I didn't have to dig very far. A note about Bill's Barbecue fluttered near the top, and I thought of the neighborhood cookout in Raleigh and felt it was finally time to learn the legend behind the landmark. The voices inside my head didn't make a peep. After that first barbecue story, I figured I had no place to go but up.

It was easy to feel intimidated walking into Bill's in search of a story. The place not only had a big reputation, it was also just plain big—a cavernous space with row after row of long tables. The set up reminded me of a popular seafood restaurant back home in Massachusetts where strangers sit elbow to elbow, prying apart clams and sucking in gook. I shook away the thought. Intimidated and grossed out are not good feelings when starting a story.

We were early, and Bill's was almost empty. I didn't see anyone in charge, so I thumped the tripod hard against the ground and the echo bounced off the walls. I made our presence known over and over again.

A man hustled up and introduced himself and introduced me to another man who at last introduced me to Bill, *the* Bill of Bill's Barbecue, a white-haired, facial-haired old-timer. His crinkly crow's feet reminded me of a NASCAR driver who'd seen a million miles out his windshield. But he eyed our camera as if it were a caution flag, and I had the feeling this TV thing was a road he hadn't traveled much.

I talked him into sitting down with me at one of those long tables and told him to start at the beginning. He said he opened his first little place in 1963. "But we went to a drive-in window and that thing was rockin' and rollin'." Bill snapped his fingers, suddenly energized by the memory. This was good. Now he looked like a country crooner with rhythmic moves and stage hair, white and wavy like George Jones, though the face was all Merle Haggard. It was lined with desperation and heartache.

Bill scraped together $500 in borrowed money and eventually opened Bill's Barbecue. Success came quickly, but so did sorrow. In one year he lost his wife, son, mother, and sister in separate, tragic circumstances. "Then turned around and lost everything else I had," he said.

He described the devastation of Hurricane Floyd that in 1999 led to the third-largest evacuation in US history. It caused $4.5 billion worth of damage along the East Coast and wiped out scores of homes and businesses, including his own. "Within two hours we had five feet of water."

He showed me a picture of his flooded restaurant, an aerial shot of a wide, flat roof in a vast gray sea. He showed me snapshots of his family, smiling faces of those who had died. I hadn't known this side of Bill's story and wasn't sure how far to probe. I've often interviewed family members who've lost loved ones and most people appreciate the opportunity to express their emotion. But this situation seemed different. I did not want Bill to cry, not *the* Bill of Bill's Barbecue, the proud legend who'd built a sprawling empire.

"See, I'm the man who started cooking on-site, taking barbecue to the people. I'm the original." Pep replaced the pain in his voice, and he pointed to a picture of an old truck. "I said, man, I'll take that thing, stick me a generator on the front, a fan on top, two fryers, and I'm ready to roll." He snapped his fingers again. "I was frying chickens as hard as I could with two fryers."

He drove his converted bread truck from coast to coast and then bought more trucks and now has a whole fleet of rigs, his name emblazoned in red on the side of each. Bill Ellis rebuilt Bill's from scratch and told me today he owns the largest catering restaurant in America, which made me think of that neighborhood cookout I went to back home in Raleigh. *Jeez, that hour drive was nothing but a hop, skip, and a jump.*

"Is there an art to making good barbecue?" I asked.

"You gotta have a good pig," he said.

"You think you have the best?"

"Well, I'll put it this way: I don't think you can get no better. Why don't you try some?"

It was getting toward lunchtime, and the staff had just set up the buffet. "Food's ready," Bill said. "Help yourself."

I walked up and looked over the long steaming spread and spooned polite scoops of barbecue and hush puppies. No need to overdo; Bill was nice enough to feed us. But then I came to the collards, and collards are good for you, right? I shoveled a decent helping and scooted back to the table.

The barbecue was hearty, the hush puppies crispy and sweet. I saved the healthy collards for last and forked a clump, but the fork wouldn't stay level on its way to my mouth. The leafy mound seemed surprisingly heavy. But when I dumped it on my tongue it sure was tasty, especially for something so green and good for you.

"Go get yourself some more," Bill said and snapped his fingers. I loved when he did that. His enthusiasm was contagious.

"Think I will," I said and skipped up to the buffet for round two and went straight for the healthy collards. This time my scoop was a little less polite. I filled most of my plate with the good green veggies and turned for my table again with a big buttery smile.

I cleaned the plate, no problem—healthy, healthy, healthy. Bill swung by just as I finished, and I thanked him for the delicious meal and told him I admired his success in the face of so much adversity. "It's a great story," I said. He smiled and the wrinkles at his mouth, crinkles by his eyes, and wavy white hair made me once again think of NASCAR. The man looked like he belonged in the winner's circle.

It was time to go, and I pushed out my chair and stood—and clung to the table for support. *Must have sat too long*, I thought, and I shook my legs, trying to get the blood flowing. But the problem was not with my legs. When I shuffled a few steps an ocean swished inside my stomach, and I swayed and lurched for the table again.

It took me three attempts and twenty minutes to waddle to the car. I buckled my seat belt and unbuckled my pants belt. My bloated belly needed room, and I needed air. I flipped the AC on full blast and wondered if a person could die from eating too many collards. I panted and closed my eyes, and who should gallop into mind but Daniel Boone.

I'd once done a story on Daniel Boone, who had lived part of his life in western North Carolina. Historians told me the great frontiersman sometimes killed twenty bears in a single day. But they also said he died from eating too many sweet potatoes. Sweet potatoes are supposed to be healthy, too.

I somehow made it back to Raleigh without leaving the collards on the side of the road. I never did find out what watery broth was in them. I just know I didn't put another thing in my mouth for two days. And I didn't eat healthy collards again for a long time. Or sweet potatoes for that matter.

But I did return to Wilson, land of good stories and friendly people. And home to another barbecue empire.

PARKER'S

I'D STOPPED AT PARKER'S BEFORE BUT WITHOUT TRYING THE barbecue, crazy as that sounds. It's like going to Disney World and skipping the Magic Kingdom. I was at Parker's, not to eat but to gather news. A hurricane had rocked a whole run of telephone poles that stretched along the street in front of the restaurant. There must have been twenty poles leaning halfway over with lots of loose and tangled wires. I hunted for somebody to interview and found a short, bald-headed manager at Parker's with an apron tied around his waist. He flicked a hand at the leaning line of timber as if to say, "Aah, that's nothin', no big deal. Just a little Mickey Mouse hurricane. No power, no problem." He told me the place would be all set for the lunch crowd and dinner, too. I figured he must have one powerful generator inside.

I've shot many stories in Wilson and have formed a good contact there who's become a friend. Keith is a photographer who used to shoot for the local newspaper and knows just about everybody in town and all the great places to eat. Weeks after the hurricane blew through, Robert and I were back for another story when Keith suggested we meet at Parker's. I called home to tell Nina I'd be late and not to worry about saving me dinner.

It was good to see all the telephone poles in their proper place and to meet the bald-headed manager again. His name was Eric. Keith had called ahead, so everything was already prepared. Eric had even ditched his apron to join us at the table for some dinner of his own. But no sooner had we sat down when he popped up and crooked a finger at me. "Come here," he said. "Wanna show you something."

He took me behind the kitchen door where people in aprons scurried about. I caught a powerful whiff of fried chicken and was tempted to snatch a drumstick, but we breezed past and left the commotion behind.

We marched through a corridor and came at last to an enormous steel door. Eric pried the latch; the handle clacked, the door swung wide, and a rush of cold air blasted me in the face. I should have shut my eyes, but not because of the cold. The fridge was full of dead hogs dangling from hooks. Eric politely introduced them with a sweep of his hand and may have even said, "Ta-da!" I nodded and tried to smile but thought of the Disney movie *Babe* about the cute talking pig and shivered instead.

We rejoined the table where Keith and Robert were feasting on hush puppies as an appetizer. Eric snatched one from the basket and bit the end like it was a cigar. He leaned back in his chair, crossed his legs, twiddled his hush puppy, and filled us in on the colorful history of the restaurant.

Two brothers and a cousin opened Parker's when Wilson's tobacco business was booming. Tobacco buyers liked the food so much that they spread the word while traveling the circuit, and the place became widely known—and it still is. The long white building has stretched along Highway 301 since 1946.

My friend Keith talked about Parker's all the time, and reviews I pulled from the Internet backed him up. I'd researched the restaurant from my office desk in Raleigh and especially got a kick out of one note:

I consider myself a BBQ connoisseur, and this place made my Top 5 globally. The pulled pork was insanely good, and the chicken was outstanding. I just may invest in hiring their chef and building an in-law suite over my garage for him. No, on second thought I'll take the in-law suite and he may have the main house!

The waitress came by with a loaded tray and we oohed and aahed before even taking a bite. Chicken, barbecue, green beans, corn bread, and another big basket of hush puppies. When we finally dug in, our oohs and aahs became a full-fledged chorus. The meat was tender and moist and full of spices.

But there's only so much oohing and aahing a reporter can do, so between bites I began to ask Eric a bit about himself, how he liked Wilson and the restaurant business. "Lot of good places to eat around here," I said and grew curious. "Where do *you* eat when you're not working?" I asked.

All forks at the table froze, and Keith, Robert, and I leaned in to listen. Eric reached in the basket, drew another hush puppy, bit off the end and eyed each of us like a poker player keeping his cards close to his vest. He broke his silence at last. "B's," he said. But the response threw me. I thought he might be bluffing.

"Bees?" I asked. "As in honey?" But he never had the chance to answer.

The clatter of silver on porcelain made me jump. "I knew it!" Keith cried. He'd dropped his fork to clap his hands, a thunder clap—Keith had big hands.

"I knew it!" He thrust his back against his chair with such force I thought he might flip over. "B's!"

"Bees?" I asked again.

Keith finally spelled it for me with his finger. "The letter," he said and drew a line and two loops in the air and began telling me all about B's Barbecue in Greenville, a tiny place without a telephone. "Can't call 'em if you wanna do a story," he said. "Just gotta show up. But show up early. They close the doors when the food runs out, and sometimes the doors close before noon."

Eric had bit the end off another hush puppy and was leaning back with his legs crossed again. "They got the best barbecue," he said and this time I had the feeling he was not bluffing—but probably should have been.

"The best barbecue?" I asked and would have dropped my fork had the plates been paper rather than porcelain.

"Second best," he quickly muttered, and popped in the whole hush puppy and sneaked a smile with his mouth full.

B'S BARBECUE

I HAD AN INKLING THE PLACE MUST BE SOMETHING SPECIAL, AND not just because the competition ate there. It was when I pulled the address off the Internet. B's Barbecue was located on B's Barbeque Road.

"A road named for the restaurant?" Robert said. "No way is that gonna show up." He sat behind the wheel of the Ford, cradling the portable navigation system. He was punching in the street name and snickering as if defying the gadget to display the address. I'm sure he was thinking no way on God's gray asphalt it would—though I hoped it did or we'd be lost. "Not a chance," he said. "B's Barbeque Road—yeah, right."

He pressed Enter, and when the monitor went blank, Robert grinned. But a moment later the screen flashed B's Barbeque Road, and he frowned. I exhaled.

As it turned out, we probably could have found the place on our own. We grabbed the Greenville exit, stopped at the first light, and voilà. "B's Barbeque Road," Robert muttered, like he was disappointed. It wasn't just a hand-carved sign either but a fancy green one with glittery letters posted above a bustling intersection. We turned left and kept our eyes peeled.

I'd heard B's was just a dinky little shack a passerby wouldn't notice if not for all the people milling around, waiting to get in. I checked my watch: 11:00 a.m. *Won't be much milling around now*, I thought. *Still early for lunch.*

Robert braked for traffic, and I spotted cars up ahead slowing and veering off the road, pulling onto the grassy bank and parking. It looked like the outside of my church on a busy Sunday. I tapped my watch and held it to my ear. *Tick, tick, tick.* It wasn't broken; the time was right. It *was* early for lunch, but all those cars—and all those people.

They stood with hands in their pockets and shirtsleeves rolled to their elbows, and just beyond them was a tiny white box of a building. The description

was dead-on. The place was about the size of a one-pump gas station, and with all the cars you would have thought there was a fuel shortage. We squeezed our Ford under a tree, and I jumped out, stricken with a sense of urgency. I remembered the warning: B's closes when the food runs out, sometimes before noon. My watch was working, all right; in fact, the hands seemed to be speeding forward. 11:10.

But Robert was rummaging around the trunk and fumbling with the microphone batteries, putting in new ones and tossing the old. *Tick, tick, tick.* My blood pressure shot skyward as the big hand aimed downward. Another minute slipped by when Robert at last said, "Ready," and we bolted for the building.

A long line snaked from the take-out window, and I did what any harried reporter would do: I cut to the front. The man leaning on the sill appeared to be waiting for the screen to slide open with his food and certainly wasn't expecting a reporter to march up with a microphone. But he said, "Sure, you can interview me," and made an attempt at straightening his tie and clapping the dust off his wing tips. He told me he was a lawyer from Greenville and stopped at B's a couple times a week. "How's the barbecue?" I asked.

"Oh, it's the best barbecue in Pitt County," he cried in a tinny voice, which made me wonder how much spicy barbecue sauce he'd guzzled over the years.

"Best barbecue in Pitt County?" I asked, egging him on.

"It may be the best barbecue in the whole world!" he whined, giving me the sound bite I was looking for.

The screen slid open and two hands poked out, gripping a bulky bag. The lawyer snatched it and hugged it to his chest as though it were the latest John Grisham novel hot off the press. He started to leave but turned back and asked the hands, "Got any extra sauce?"

I started to turn away, too, but a big man wandered up with his chin out. "Oh, this hasn't gotten busy yet," he said, and I gathered he was a B's Barbecue professional. He spoke like he wanted it to get busy—except he'd stepped out of line to talk to me and realized he'd lost his place. He tucked in his chin and sneaked a smile. "Oh, well," he said and shuffled to the back. He was a good sport, and I think he enjoyed standing in line, anticipating the meal ahead and talking to folks in front of him. I grinned when I saw him stick out his chin again and engage a lady in conversation.

There were several picnic tables outside B's, and I interviewed a banker on his lunch break at one of them. His white shirt helped hide his perspiration, but the red sauce threatened his tie, and so he'd flung it over his shoulder. "It's the best," he garbled. His plate was half empty, his mouth stuffed full.

I checked my watch—11:35—and eyed the front door, which stood wide open, lucky for us. Time to find out what exactly was inside that little building—before the food ran out.

I walked in and ducked my head even though I'm barely five foot six on a good day. It wasn't just that the ceiling was low, but lots of bulky duct work hung from it. I'm not sure what wafted through those dented metal boxes, but it wasn't air-conditioning. B's was famous for not having AC. A lonely fan, jammed between the open window and sill, barely made a dent; its aluminum frame was flecked with rust and rattled continuously. The temperature inside that July day might have been close to triple digits, but people I talked with seemed almost proud of the heat. Good barbecue came with sacrifice and sweat.

B's was also famous for not having a telephone, and the restaurant's faithful seemed proud of that, too. I noticed people didn't even talk on their cell phones. It just wasn't a cell phone kind of place.

> B'S WAS ALSO FAMOUS FOR NOT HAVING A TELEPHONE, AND THE RESTAURANT'S FAITHFUL SEEMED PROUD OF THAT, TOO. I NOTICED PEOPLE DIDN'T EVEN TALK ON THEIR CELL PHONES. IT JUST WASN'T A CELL PHONE KIND OF PLACE.

It was a Robert kind of place. He's a photographer who doesn't trust technology, including navigation systems, but give him a good hole-in-the wall and he'll jump right in. He began shooting everything in sight, though it was too bad the camera couldn't capture the smells. Body odor was one of them, but the sweet spicy scent of barbecue overwhelmed even that.

"Number one," said a man holding up his index finger. "It's the best." His finger was aimed at the duct work but I don't think that's what he meant. "There's no other barbecue like B's."

I saw an older woman push her hands through the loops of two plastic bags and carry them on her forearms, hunching as she walked. She was a small woman, and when the load swayed I feared she might tilt and fall. I offered to give her a hand, but she asked for the microphone instead, apparently glad to talk and rest a moment.

"How crowded does it get?" I asked.

"Oh, my God," she said. "You gotta spend the night to get some chicken." She cracked a smile and shuffled past, bags swaying, and made it out the door.

What I noticed about B's, other than how hot and crowded it was, were all the different types of people: black, white, young, old, business pros, and

blue-collar folks, and they all seemed to be enjoying both their food and each other. Of course, in a place that small you couldn't help but rub elbows with a stranger.

"They're like family," said the woman behind the counter, nodding her head at the crowd. She clamped her hands to her hips and blew a strand of hair from her eyes. Her name was Tammy, and she told me her daddy opened B's in 1978. "Just on a whim, and we've been going ever since." Her dad was William MacLawhorn, who'd since passed away, and now Tammy and her sisters were making a go of what he'd started. "His spirit is in this place," she said. "He's here every day even though he's not." Her gaze drifted over my shoulder. "It means a lot," she said more to herself than me. "We're very proud of it."

I turned and took in the room myself. People leaned over their plates or tipped their cups or talked and laughed, and I watched them like watching a movie, off to the side but absorbed by everything I saw and heard. The place had a kind of rhythmic murmur that draped over me like a warm quilt. Or maybe it was the scent that was so comforting, which seemed to soak through my skin like a salve.

A loud clang behind me broke my trance and I turned around again. Tammy had slid the lid off a metal container and was peering into it and frowning.

"Almost out of chicken!" she hollered to the cook. I looked too, but not to see how many chickens were left. It was my watch I checked. Both hands pointed straight up. High noon!

I told Robert to shoot like the wind, fast and furious, which made me think of the rattling fan more or less spinning in its tracks. "Shoot the fan," I told him, because I knew I'd mention it in my script. No AC and no phone gave the place character. Plus, I'd picked up a few factoids. I'd learned the night-owl crew slow-cooked pigs in the wee hours, usually eight pigs a day but a dozen or more on game days during football and basketball season. And still the place often sold out by noon.

"You gotta eat," Tammy said and hurried me to a booth. She asked the man sitting there to make room. "Got another one joining you." The man waved his fork, *C'mon*, and scooted over. He told me he ate at B's all the time.

"Best barbecue I ever had," he said.

But reporters are skeptical, especially those used to eating hot dogs and hamburgers. When Tammy delivered my barbecue sandwich, it could have been peanut butter and jelly as far as I was concerned. I like PB&J, but one is just like another.

I took a bite, and the barbecue hadn't even tumbled down my throat when the flavor hit me like a blast of cool air from the window fan—totally unexpected. Meaty, moist, and seasoned to perfection. Absolutely delicious. I devoured it and would have sprung for seconds but figured the door would be closing any minute.

I sat there considering everything that was packed between the walls: so many good people and such rich tradition and the whole place chock-full of character. I figured about the only thing our camera hadn't captured was the chicken. "That's it! We're out!" Tammy hollered.

I checked my watch—it was getting late—and I found myself wishing time could slow down or stop altogether. But then again there was always next time, another trip to B's, maybe on my own time next time when I wasn't working. I'd order barbecue *and* chicken. But I'd have to arrive early. Well before noon. Before the door closed.

PIK N PIG

WELL, I'D DONE IT. I'D PLUNGED INTO BARBECUE WHOLE HOG, AND now every barbecue story that came my way was fair game, no turning back. *You want the best BBQ in North Carolina?* the e-mails often read. *We got it. Come on!*

I admired all those notes—me, a hot dog eater—and found myself pulled to the other side, the barbecue side, by the eastern side and western side, both sides urging me to visit their little towns and try their delicious pig. But which pig to pick next? I picked the Pik N Pig.

When I think of Moore County I think Southern Pines and Pinehurst, golf courses, and money. But Carthage is in Moore County, too, and its claim to fame is the horse and buggy. It was once the buggy capital of the South.

At its height, the Tyson & Jones Buggy Company turned out three thousand buggies and carriages a year. It was known for building the Cadillac of buggies, and royalty from overseas would sometimes visit to see their deluxe models being made. Tyson & Jones supposedly became the first factory in the nation to adopt an assembly-line manufacturing system.

According to legend, a young entrepreneur visited the factory in the early 1900s and was struck with a profound idea: convert it to build cars. "Cars?" said the horse-and-buggy folks. They rejected his offer, and he returned home to Detroit to set up shop there. The man's name was Henry Ford.

Today Carthage is a quiet town with little evidence of its missed opportunity in history. The buggy company closed in 1925 and then caught fire, and the small part that survived is now an antique store. But Carthage does hold a buggy festival every year and is proud of its contribution to transportation.

That contribution extends to a runway outside a popular barbecue restaurant. When I heard about the odd combination—planes and pigs—I didn't exactly picture sleek jets and well-to-do pilots but figured it must be a

single-engine Cessna crowd wobbling in for some good grub. My kind of folks and one unique story.

The e-mails I received said the restaurant sat right next to the runway: *Eat and watch the planes. So close you can practically touch 'em!* I called the Pik N Pig to make sure it was true.

"How far exactly *is* the runway from the restaurant?" I asked.

"Oh, few feet," said the man on the line. "Not far."

I suppose I should have asked if a wing had ever clipped the dining room, but what I said instead was, "We plan to stop by Friday. Think you'll have many folks flying in?"

"Don't know," he said and after a long pause added, "I'll see what I can do," which sounded only faintly promising. From my perspective—and the camera's—the more planes the better.

When Friday arrived so did my doubts. I just couldn't imagine many pilots forking out hundreds or even thousands of dollars in fuel to fly in and eat ten dollars' worth of barbecue, no matter how delicious it was. My only hope was that the man on the phone had called around—maybe he was a bit more forward thinking than the folks from the horse-and-buggy factory had been a hundred years before.

But my hopes soared when we veered onto a dusty lane that opened to a grassy field with a rambling brown building in the distance and a sunny sky filled with flying machines, more planes than I could have ever dreamed. You would have thought it was the Fourth of July at Kitty Hawk.

We found a parking space and jumped out and raced for the runway, which really was just a few feet from the restaurant. I ducked as I ran.

Planes were taxiing every which way, and I made sure to stop well shy of the propellers but close enough for the pilots to see me waving my notepad. One had just parked his single seater and was climbing out. I shouted to him, "No, stay right there," and hoisted myself onto the wing and snaked the mic around his neck.

"I have a passion for flying," he said once I jumped back down.

"Do you have a passion for barbecue?"

He laughed and patted the fuselage. "I have a passion for barbecue, and that's why this is a good mix." It *was* a good mix, both his laugh and his fuselage pat, which made for a nice touch.

We were in good position to capture the planes—landing, taxiing, and taking off. I clamped my hands over my ears and struggled to keep my balance. *VROOOOOM!* and *WHOOOOOSH!*

"It's more fun than you can imagine," said another pilot. "We can't wipe the grin off our faces." He climbed from the cockpit and headed for the restaurant, helmet in hand, chin strap swinging with his step.

I couldn't wait to thank the person who'd orchestrated this fly-in bonanza, the man on the phone no doubt, and after teetering by the runway a while—*VROOOOOM!*—I turned for the Pik N Pig.

Roland Gilliam was there to greet me, a barrel-chested man in a denim shirt and gray hair beneath his faded blue hat. The crinkles by his eyes made me think he must have peered into many a sunlit sky. To me he was the exact vision of a veteran aviator.

"I always wanted my own airport, so I started building me an airport," he said. We sat at the outdoor eating area, which made for a great shot with all those planes in the background.

"Is it a restaurant with an airstrip or an airstrip with a restaurant?" I asked.

"Well, the airstrip came first."

He told me he built it in 1994, and the place took off. *VROOOOOM! WHOOOOOSH!* Another plane roared by, and my hair spray didn't stand a chance.

Roland said pilots flew in from all over. "There's a man from Cincinnati, Ohio," he said. "He's flying in tomorrow to eat, all the way from Cincinnati."

I flipped open my pad. *Holy Toledo!* I wrote.

I would have kept sitting and talking and enjoying the view if not for two ladies nearby who seemed to be enjoying it more.

"Look, look!" one of them exclaimed.

"Oh, my gosh!" cried the other.

The ladies lounged in Adirondack chairs, heads tilted back, eyes on the skies. "Oh, my!" they shouted at once and giggled and kicked their feet like little children. I knew this was an interview opportunity I couldn't let pass. I quickly thanked Roland, stood, and made for the Adirondack ladies.

"Oh, here he comes," they squealed, but they weren't talking about me. *WHOOOOOSH!* The plane blew past just a few feet above the runway, and I suspected the pilot was showing off. The ladies were eating it up. They waved and kicked and shouted above the roar. "Oh, that is magnificent!"

They were so cute and absorbed in the action that when I clipped on the mics they barely paid me any mind. I stepped back and let them rip. *VROOOOOM!* "Whoo, hoo!" piped one of them.

"That deserves a ten!" exclaimed the other. If only they had little chalkboards to score the pilots, but I wasn't about to be greedy. The Adirondack ladies were sensational as it was.

"Wonder what the barbecue does to their tummies?" one asked.

"Maybe the gas quotient changes," said the other, and they both busted out in laughter—I just hoped the sound bite would win my editor's approval.

I think the ladies had forgotten they were wearing microphones until I approached again. "Isn't this incredible?" one of them said, handing me back the mic. But the other Adirondack lady answered in my place.

"It just doesn't get any better than this!"

The Pik N Pig was a story with two halves. We'd captured the planes. Now we needed the barbecue.

I TURNED FOR THE RESTAURANT DOOR BUT TOOK ANOTHER MINUTE TO LOOK AROUND BEFORE GOING IN. PLANES WERE EVERYWHERE, CIRCLING OVERHEAD AND LEAVING PUFFY TRAILS STRETCHING ACROSS THE SKY, BRIGHT WHITE AGAINST A BACKDROP OF CAROLINA BLUE. BEAUTIFUL, I THOUGHT. THE PLACE WAS ALIVE, BOTH ABOVE AND BELOW.

I found the cook around back by the grill, a lanky rubber band of a man who looked like he either skipped meals or sweated them out. He lifted the grill's hooded top and waved away the smoke to show me the goods. Chunks of meat the color of mahogany roasted on several racks. "Live coals, no gas, no electricity," he said and told me he'd save me some. I thanked him and hoped he was going to save some for himself, too. The man needed meat on his ribs.

I turned for the restaurant door but took another minute to look around before going in. Planes were everywhere, circling overhead and leaving puffy trails stretching across the sky, bright white against a backdrop of Carolina blue. *Beautiful*, I thought. The place was alive, both above and below. Planes swooped in and touched down, and the roar and groan of the engines only added to the buzz.

I noticed a family leaning against a split-rail fence, taking it all in. "A restaurant with an airstrip," said the man I took to be the dad.

"Probably the only one," the gray-haired grandma said.

As electric as the atmosphere was, I was glad to finally slip inside. Two hours in the hot sun at the edge of a busy runway had me feeling as whipped as a windsock.

The restaurant was full of heavy wood, which made the room dark despite the big window that offered diners a bird's-eye view of the action outside. I figured the window must be extra thick because it certainly dulled the noise beyond it. It was almost like watching a silent movie.

I ordered and ate, and my compliments to the cook. Cooked to perfection. The barbecue tasted as good as it had looked on the racks, and I appreciated the effort that went into it.

I enjoyed savoring my meal and looking out at the planes and thinking about the Wright brothers and Henry Ford and the horse-and-buggy days of Carthage. What if Henry Ford *had* bought that old buggy factory in town? It would have changed not only Carthage but North Carolina and might have altered the whole history of the country. *Missed opportunity?* I mused. I supposed that was one way to look at it. And yet I couldn't help feeling grateful that Carthage had remained a quaint little town, proud of its history while embracing its energy, and there was plenty of that outside the window.

I tracked a plane across the sky and watched it dip down and aim for the runway. The pilot tilted the wings left, then right as if waving to the crowd and dipped lower still, but instead of touching down he throttled hard at the last moment and shot skyward again, a dazzling aeronautic display right outside the window.

Boy, I thought, *sure hope the Adirondack ladies saw that one. No doubt about it. Definitely a ten!*

WILBER'S BARBECUE
(AND THE MISSING BOMB)

WILBER'S SITS ALONG HIGHWAY 70 IN GOLDSBORO. IT HAS BEEN around for fifty years. And it might have come within a hog's whisker of being blown to smithereens.

"He likes the barbecue, but he loves the hot dogs," said a lady at a table with her grandson. *Hot dogs?* I thought. *At the most famous barbecue restaurant in North Carolina?* But the kid was irresistible. I smiled at his chubby cheeks smeared with ketchup. "My family's been coming to Wilber's for years," said Grandma. "Three generations. Love the barbecue!" She was giving me good sound bites, but I couldn't take my eyes off the kid. He pinched a chunk of dog between his messy fingers and popped it in his mouth and didn't even give Grandma and me a glance when we laughed. He was already reaching for another chunk, oblivious to the ketchup at the end of his nose.

Fifteen miles from Wilber's rests a hydrogen bomb two hundred feet beneath a muddy cornfield. It's Wayne County's other claim to fame—or claim to infamy. The bomb has not yet exploded.

The sun beat down, not a cloud overhead, and a chatty crowd happily hob-nobbed on a corner in downtown Eureka—in Eureka the corner pretty much *is* the downtown. Robert and I trotted across the street into the merry huddle, accepting warm handshakes and pats on the back. Folks were thrilled we'd come to cover the big event—the big reveal. They collected around a tall pole draped with a black sheet, but at the moment nobody seemed a bit curious about it. The whole gathering reminded me of a class reunion with giddy locals swapping fond memories. And sharing stories about the night the bomb dropped.

Wayne County marked two milestones in July 2012: Wilber's Barbecue was turning fifty, and the county was dedicating a historical marker to the missing bomb. Wilber's had helped put Wayne County on the map. The bomb had nearly wiped it off the map.

That day in early July, Robert and I jumped on I-70 with coffee to go and a plan. We'd cover the marker dedication in the morning, then scoot to Wilber's for the lunch crowd. Wilber's fiftieth anniversary party wasn't for two more weeks, but we'd shoot the story now and air it later.

Our route took us by Wilber's on the way to the marker, and Robert tapped the brake, tempted I'm sure to veer in, uncrumple a few bills, and snag a barbecue sandwich for the rest of the ride. The place is a low brick building with white trim, nothing fancy about it and no indication of the landmark it is, except maybe for all the cars packing the lot. And the traffic thundering overhead.

An F-15 screamed across our windshield, rattling our Taurus.

Wilber's sits in the shadow of Seymour Johnson Air Force Base. I'd been here before and knew jets routinely roared over the roof. I had admired the planes and sampled the barbecue, and I thought Robert's stomach was probably growling, but not for a snack anymore. I think he was busting a gut to grab the camera and fire some shots at the F-15 before it disappeared on the

horizon. But the clock grabbed our attention, too, and we couldn't afford to watch time vanish either. So we rolled on in hopes of catching some planes later.

We actually arrived early for the big reveal in Eureka, twenty minutes north of Wilber's, and it felt good mingling with all those friendly folks around the pole. There was energy in the air. But, of course, it was the energy underground that had brought everybody together. The bomb was tucked deep in a cornfield one crossroad over, three miles down the road in a little community called Faro. *Plenty close enough*, I thought. In fact, it wouldn't have bothered me if the state had plunked the marker one whole county over.

Our camera was easy to spot, and the event organizer grabbed my arm and hustled me through the crowd, hollering over his shoulder that he was taking me to a fella who could tell me everything I wanted to know. "In *Reader's Digest* fashion!" he bellowed.

"Perfect," I shouted back while dodging elbows.

He passed me off to a tall man with a scruffy beard and floppy hat. "If that thing had detonated, it would have made a one-hundred-percent kill zone of seventeen miles," he said, and I chewed the inside of my cheek to keep from grinning. Nothing like a whopper of a sound bite to kick things off. This guy was gonna be good. He'd written a book about the missing bomb but looked nothing at all like an expert. The floppy hat was sensational.

Joel Dobson was eager to take me back to January 1961 when fighter planes patrolled the Atlantic twenty-four hours a day. "That was a period of time when America was terrified of the Soviet Union," he said and launched into the story.

He told me late one night an armed B-52 began leaking fuel from its right wing—thirty-seven thousand pounds of fuel in three minutes. The bomber aimed for the nearest runway: Seymour Johnson Air Force Base in Goldsboro. But twelve miles out and thousands of feet up all hell broke loose. And so did the B-52.

"The right wing of this aircraft folded up and came off the airplane," Joel said and jerked his arm to illustrate how catastrophic it was. The arm jerk was great television. He looked like he was doing the chicken dance. "It completely came off the airplane, and then the airplane disintegrated."

The plane carried two bombs, three-and-a-half megatons a piece. "Three-and-a-half megatons equate to two hundred sixty-four Hiroshima bombs," Joel said and paused a beat—a couple seconds of silence can be great television, too. Then he lowered the boom. "So we had the equivalent of five hundred Hiroshima bombs falling on Faro." Man, this guy was more than good.

One of the bombs gently parachuted down. But the other one . . . "The parachute did not open," he said and held my gaze. "And it hit the ground traveling seven hundred miles an hour."

"What happened?" I said, slightly breathless, even though I'd researched the event and knew the outcome.

Joel launched into a bit of nuclear gobbledygook, fortunately in the promised *Reader's Digest* fashion. He told me the bomb came equipped with six arming mechanisms and that five of them activated. In other words, one little switch kept the bomb from blowing everything to high heaven. "One notch from having one big lake in eastern North Carolina."

But instead of *BOOM*, the bomb went *splat,* and within an hour Air Force officials were hauling tail down Big Daddy's Road and crawling all over the muddy cornfield beside it. They found a crewman's body hanging from a tree, his neck broken. Two others also died, and five ejected safely.

Joel painted a vivid picture of the scene: fire and smoke and wreckage scattered two miles wide. He talked faster as he went. He told me the debris included pieces of the bomb, which disintegrated on impact—except for the part that *whomped* into the mud. "Jeez," I said.

The local power company mounted lights, and teams frantically searched the smoldering crater. They dug all night, but the hole kept filling with water from a nearby swamp. So the Air Force hauled in sixteen pumps and bailed out twenty thousand gallons of water, but still the hole filled, and the sun rose and set and rose again.

I had made a decision. I was definitely going to buy Joel's book—even though I knew the ending.

Teams toiled for five months before finally giving up and leaving the buried bomb. Or at least part of the bomb—its uranium core. I asked another historian what uranium does. "It goes boom," he said rather candidly, and I thought, *Whoa, this guy's about as good as Joel.* "A lot of people thought it was gonna be the end of time."

"Is there a danger today?" I asked—talk about a loaded question.

"No," he said quite emphatically, and to tell the truth I wasn't sure if I was relieved or disappointed. "Yes" would have made great TV.

He explained that experts were satisfied the bomb posed no threat, but in the same breath he told me the Army Corps of Engineers purchased an easement around the land so the property can never be developed and that scientists test the water even today to make sure it's not contaminated. I was beginning to wish the state had erected the marker as far away as Raleigh.

"We give thanks unto thee and thy guidance that a catastrophe did not happen." The ceremony began with a preacher at the lectern, his head bowed and hands folded across his chest. The chitter-chatter was over, and the mood turned somber as one witness after another described what they saw that night.

"There was wreckage burning across the highway," said a man, urgency in his voice fifty-one years later—and in his body, too. He trembled. "And they told us, 'Move on.' Said, 'People, for God's sake, get outta here!'"

Even team members who'd dug for the bomb had returned for the marker dedication. "The weapon is about the size of this propane tank," said the squad's retired commander. The tank he pointed to was a three-foot-long canister outside the reception building, where ladies were inside heating up fried chicken and biscuits for the ceremony after-party. "It buried itself in the ground and ended up in kind of a J position"—as opposed to an O position that might have been easier to extract. He also said it had been damn close to exploding, with particular emphasis on "damn."

Also returning was the B-52's relief pilot, one of the men who'd parachuted just in time. "I'm grateful to God," Adam Mattocks said and moved through the crowd shaking hands, a bit unsteady because of his age. Pleased to meet all of you," he said softly, "and I thank you for your effort." People gripped his hand with both of theirs.

The dignitaries concluded the ceremony by tugging at the black sheet, which stubbornly clung to the corner of the maker, but people didn't seem impatient. I suppose they'd learned to keep calm after living half a century with a hydrogen bomb in their backyard.

When the sheet finally slipped away folks clapped and tilted their heads at the big metal plaque, headlined NUCLEAR MISHAP in large capital letters. They seemed proud of the sign—or proud they'd survived. The marker was a badge of honor, their medal for bravery.

But to me, the greater drama was in the smaller text inscribed below: WIDE-SPREAD DISASTER AVERTED.

It's difficult to immediately hop from one story to the next. The tentacles of my brain wouldn't let go of the bomb as we pulled into the parking lot at Wilber's. Even the promise of world-famous barbecue couldn't shake them loose. I climbed from the car with my head still wrapped around the interviews we'd gathered in Eureka, grappling with some sort of story outline. And then the air exploded.

A sleek-nosed silver bomber thundered low across my eyes, loud and impressive, and I thought how different from the bulky B-52 that "mishapped" over Faro. The roar rippled through me, and that did the trick. The tentacles fell away, and I realized the potential staring me in the face, both overhead and on the ground: brute force hurtling over southern hospitality. *Now that's a pretty good story*, I thought, and tucked the bomb in my mental compartment and readied my brain and belly for barbecue.

But first things first. Robert clamped the camera to the tripod and aimed at the sky, and every few minutes another jet screamed past—probably just routine training for the F-15s, but a photographer couldn't have asked for a more dramatic shot. He even angled his camera to catch Wilber's American flag waving in the foreground as another bomber bit the sky.

Wilber's was my kind of place. The inside was paneled with lots of warm wood that reminded me of the cozy den of my boyhood home. I used to sneak away in there as a kid and curl in the rocker by the fireplace or flip through leather-bound encyclopedias that lined three shelves of our bookcase. Wilber's had the feel of a place where you just wanted to take a load off, while away time, and savor good 'cue and conversation. Or enjoy a hot dog rolled in ketchup.

I was off to a great start with the little boy and his grandma. Cute kids make great TV—but company officials, not so much. And yet I couldn't ignore the sign on the wall that read BOARD OF DIRECTORS TABLE and the long row of chatty folks seated across from it.

"I just enjoy being here," said a lady board member in a flowered dress, which seemed a little formal in a laid-back place like Wilber's, but she apparently took her board duty seriously even though it wasn't serious at all. The sign was in jest, the "Board of Directors" a regular social circle. "I eat here twice a day almost every day."

"Twice a day? Really?"

"Yes, sir," she said, lifting her chin high as another plane rumbled over the restaurant. I could hear the pride in her voice and feel it in the air. But I had to listen closely. The cacophony inside tended to dampen the thunder outside.

WILBER'S WAS MY KIND OF PLACE. THE INSIDE WAS PANELED WITH LOTS OF WARM WOOD THAT REMINDED ME OF THE COZY DEN OF MY BOYHOOD HOME. . . . WILBER'S HAD THE FEEL OF A PLACE WHERE YOU JUST WANTED TO TAKE A LOAD OFF, WHILE AWAY TIME, AND SAVOR GOOD 'CUE AND CONVERSATION. OR ENJOY A HOT DOG ROLLED IN KETCHUP.

"That's freedom, my friend," said a fellow board member who pointed his finger at the rafters. His weathered face made him look like an old veteran himself. "Freedom," he repeated, and he pursed his lips for full effect.

The moment of stony seriousness passed quickly, and the table soon broke into good-natured kidding with lots of funny one-liners and laughs, and we made sure to capture that, too.

I roamed the restaurant, interviewing customers, cooks, and waitresses.

"How busy do you get?"

"Oh, it's crazy."

"How's the barbecue?"

"The best."

"Tell me about Wilber."

"He's known worldwide. Very famous to be such a plain ol' country boy. I love him to death. And he'd kill me for saying this, but he's a kind-hearted soul. Did you know he's been teaching Sunday school for forty-five years?"

I'd learned through my interviews that Wilber was also wise in the ways of politics. Former governors and lawmakers were good friends, and he'd even hosted a US president or two.

"Gettin' everything you need?" I turned to face a man I recognized from the restaurant brochure. "Wilber Shirley," said Wilber, and he shook my hand. "Glad to have you."

He spoke softly; his whole manner was quiet, his complexion tanned and leathery. He wore a red shirt with WILBER'S embroidered on the front pocket and peered at me behind glasses. The more we talked the more I sensed he was thinking two steps ahead. I had a feeling it was no accident he'd waited to introduce himself. A man wise in the ways of politics knew something about strategy and timing, when to leave a camera crew alone, and when to maneuver in and lend some friendly guidance. "Interview anybody you'd like," he said.

"Well, actually," I told him, "we need to interview you." But I think he already knew that.

"Come on," he said and turned and pushed open the kitchen door and led me all the way outside, out back to an out building. "The smokehouse," he said, which was a squatty brick rectangle with a roof stuck on top. "Come on," he repeated and swung open the screen door.

It was dark inside with the sooty smell of burned-out fire. Wilber told me the cooks cooked all night and slept during the day. The place was empty except for us, and I felt like I was invading the sanctity of somebody else's man cave. This is where the deal was done, meat cooked on metal racks propped over hot coals. "We cook it all with wood," Wilber said. "Original way I learned it." I noticed he lifted his chin, too, as he spoke, and I remembered what a couple of customers had told me inside.

"It's done the hard way, but it's the right way. It's the old way."

"Ain't barbecue if it ain't cooked with wood."

I felt we'd lingered long enough and asked Wilber if we could sit down a minute. We wove back through the restaurant and found a quiet corner.

"I'm just a plain ol' country boy," were the first words out of his mouth. He pointed to an old photo on the wall that showed a young boy standing next to a mule with a bundle on its back. "That's me hauling tobacco to the barn," he said and told me about growing up hard in eastern North Carolina. Opening the restaurant fifty years ago was a chance at making enough money to get by. But Wilber's Barbecue took off—not unlike the Seymour Johnson jets. Although Wilber had stayed grounded.

"I tell everybody I didn't come out here to make a lot of money. I came to make a lot of friends. And other than that, I've just enjoyed the journey."

I didn't sit with Wilber long. I knew he enjoyed making the rounds of the restaurant. And my own journey was at an end anyway.

Before I left, Wilber fixed me a plate of his tender barbecue and moist hush puppies, and he packed a take-out box for Robert who'd hustled outside for more shots of the planes—he couldn't get enough of them.

I spotted Robert across the parking lot with his eye to the lens, smiling as he was shooting—though I was wincing. The sky was exploding again, and I turned to see another jet rip across the roof.

But in my mind's eye I found myself superimposing that sleek silver bullet with the bulky B-52 over Faro. How different the planes and times. But how similar the stories.

We'd shot Wilber's Barbecue and the missing bomb and, I thought, had captured a slice of small-town America in both, the friendliness of the people and compassion they showed for others. They enjoyed good barbecue and get-togethers and were comfortable in their surroundings and secure in their identity. And somehow that security had grown stronger when the hydrogen bomb tumbled out of the plane. When the bomb sank, community pride surfaced. And continued to soar.

What a sight. I even saluted the silver bullet as it hurtled toward the distant horizon. Life went on in Wayne County with uranium underfoot and F-15s overhead.

And the flag over Wilber's waved.

CLYDE COOPER'S BARBECUE

IN OCTOBER 2013 RALEIGH HOSTED A MAJOR BLUEGRASS FESTIVAL that drew banjo pickers, mandolin players, and scores of talented musicians from across the country. They picked and grinned up and down Fayetteville Street and on stages all over downtown. The celebration attracted more than one hundred thousand spectators who clapped their hands and tapped their toes. The music was fun, the weather perfect, and the atmosphere alive.

WRAL helped sponsor the festival and asked me to emcee one of the downtown stages on a Saturday afternoon. I was happy to because I wanted to see some of the bands myself—although I'd already been hearing banjo twangs in my head for weeks. I'd put together a thirty-minute Tar Heel Traveler special about bluegrass and its deep North Carolina roots. Robert and I had made multiple trips to the mountains, listening in on jam sessions and interviewing folks whose hearts and souls were tied to the music. Bluegrass was in their blood, a proud part of their family heritage.

The special proved to be an education for me. I normally tune the radio to classic rock and play drums on the steering wheel. But no drums in bluegrass? I hadn't thought about it till we started shooting the jam sessions and realized it was the stringed instruments that provided the beat. *But those instruments*, I wondered. *What the heck's a Dobro? And what's the difference between a fiddle and violin?*

Fortunately, Robert's wife is a music teacher who joined us on a shoot and hollered over the pickers that there really was no difference. "Good to know," I said, bobbing my head to the melody. "Band sounds great," I added, getting into the spirit. "Love me some bluegrass!"

She scrunched her face and hollered again. "This isn't bluegrass," she said. "It's old-time. There *is* a difference."

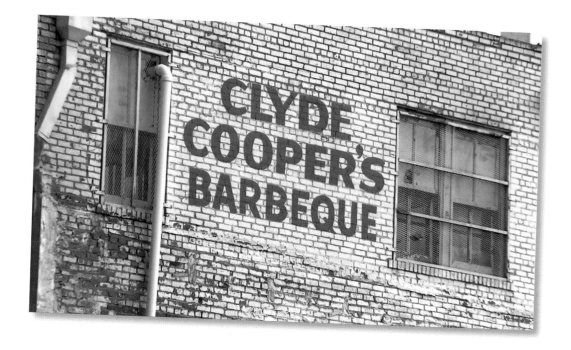

I stopped bobbing and quickly learned my lesson about bluegrass and old-time. Old-time came first, which is one difference and the easiest to explain—there's a fine line between the two. Robert's wife filled me in. And she also told me what a Dobro is.

By the Saturday afternoon of the festival, I was full of confidence and stepped right up on stage in front of all those people and spoke into the microphone about bluegrass and old-time and the rich legacy of both and then turned and introduced the band with a theatrical wave before jumping down. I'd brought my wife and kids, and we listened a while before we all started getting hungry. "Isn't Cooper's around here," Nina asked?

Of course I knew Cooper's. Everybody knows Cooper's. The place is a Raleigh landmark. People talk about Cooper's Barbecue all the time. But I had never been.

"Uh, think it's around here," I said, standing on tiptoe, seeing nothing but a swaying mass and feeling my confidence fade like the end of a song.

Nina asked directions, and in five minutes we rounded the corner onto Davie Street and spotted the brick building with the green awning. It was midafternoon by then, and we found enough empty seats in a row at the counter.

The waitress smiled and handed us menus. "How ya'll doin' today? Sweet tea?" She was southern through and through with a sugary drawl and pleasantly plump cheeks that just about squeezed her eyes shut every time she smiled—and she always smiled. She was a sweetie pie who called us "honey" and "baby" and brought us iced teas and Diet Cokes and moved slowly but happily, patiently shuffling from the prep area to the counter with a basket of hush puppies and bottles of barbecue sauce because it's a given, I suppose, that first-timers at Cooper's always order barbecue, and no doubt she knew we were first-timers. I bet she'd been shuffling the same floor for half her life and never forgot a face—or the iced tea. She topped me off when I was still two-thirds full. "Ya'll ready to order, baby?" I could have listened to her all day.

We ordered barbecue sandwiches, except for Scout, my eleven-year-old. Scout ordered a large rack of ribs and, oh how that tickled Sweetie Pie's funny bone. She leaned back and laughed, and her cheeks plumped out and her eyes closed and Scout got to laughing, too. "Sure you can eat all that, honey?" she finally asked when her eyeballs appeared, but she was already shuffling to fetch the order before Scout nodded his head *yeah*. I suppose she never forgot a first-timer's response either, especially a growing boy's.

Cooper's was old but comfortable, comfortable old like my grandmother's den with the easy chair she kept covered with a bedsheet so the fabric wouldn't get dirty. I never knew what color the chair was but loved lounging in that little room at the end of the house. I loved lounging at Cooper's, too.

I think of Cooper's as yellow, forty-watt-lightbulb yellow, the dim glow from a single ceiling bulb that has somehow burned for years. I liked the soft glow and the black-and-white photographs scattered around the walls. Cooper's had history—I could see it and feel it. Nobody had to tell me it was a landmark. I knew the linoleum under my elbows had propped a million elbows before mine, and even though the place was half empty that time of day, I had no trouble imagining

THE WAITRESS SMILED AND HANDED US MENUS. "HOW YA'LL DOIN' TODAY? SWEET TEA?" SHE WAS SOUTHERN THROUGH AND THROUGH WITH A SUGARY DRAWL AND PLEASANTLY PLUMP CHEEKS THAT JUST ABOUT SQUEEZED HER EYES SHUT EVERY TIME SHE SMILED—AND SHE ALWAYS SMILED. SHE WAS A SWEETIE PIE WHO CALLED US "HONEY" AND "BABY" AND BROUGHT US ICED TEAS AND DIET COKES AND MOVED SLOWLY BUT HAPPILY. . . .

a crowd of regulars bent over barbecue plates and—why not?—licking all ten fingers, including thumbs. Good to the last shred.

I admit I felt like a newsman who'd been wearing a potato sack over his head. *Why haven't I ever done a story on this place?* I thought. *Can't believe I've never been here before.* I hid my face in my iced-tea cup when I saw the owner walking my way. I just knew she was the owner and that she recognized the Tar Heel Traveler—who hadn't traveled to downtown Raleigh nearly enough.

"Well, hello there," she said, and I gulped and wiped my chin with the back of my hand and then wiped it on my pants when she offered to shake.

Debbie Holt was a talkative blonde who told me about Clyde Cooper, who sure could cook up some barbecue, and how Cooper's Barbecue had been serving Clyde Cooper's recipe since 1938. "Seventy-five years," she said, which was like two big pokes to my potato sack, punching eye holes in the burlap. *That's the hook,* I thought. *Seventy-five years.* Except in two months it would be seventy-six years. I'd have to turn the story before the calendar flipped to 2014. I told Debbie I'd definitely be calling soon. Shoot, if Robert had been around I would have done the story right then and there. But I was due back on stage in—*twenty minutes!*

"Gotta go," I told the family and ate my sandwich on the run. I tried to rehearse my bluegrass spiel as I darted between people on the street but couldn't shake my visit to Cooper's. The place was still on my skin—I licked my fingers along the way—and I couldn't wait to return soon with the camera. I was also itching to find out if Scout had managed to finish his rack of ribs. I pictured Sweetie Pie watching him and laughing again, cheeks puffed, eyes closed. And, boy, was I glad mine had been opened.

I was back two weeks later with Robert, and it was like sitting in on one of those pickin' and grinnin' sessions. I knew it was special. The beat felt right, and the place was humming. The counter was full, the booths were full, and so were the walls—and not just with old photographs. I studied the walls a little more this time and chuckled at T-shirts spread wide with their sleeves pinned. The shirts bore a fat picture of a pig's rump, and on a chunky cheek beside its curly-cue tail was 75TH ANNIVERSARY stamped inside a circle. The hog's fanny was priceless. It was the first thing Robert shot.

The first person we interviewed was Debbie, the talkative owner. "People come in here and go all around and look at the pictures." She turned 180 degrees. "They just love the oldness of it." *Bull's-eye,* I thought, knowing exactly what she meant. "Evidently the man was doing something right, because it's here for seventy-five years, so, yeah, you don't mess with what's not broken."

The man she was talking about of course was Clyde Cooper, whose picture was all over the walls, too. I studied the nearest one and admired a trim man in suit and tie standing at the head of the counter with his white-shirted staff lined up next to him. He had a long face and easy smile and looked like somebody about to sit down to Sunday dinner after church.

Debbie had known Clyde from when she'd worked at the restaurant in the early '90s. She told me he was the son of a dairy farmer and that he borrowed $2,000 from his brother to buy the restaurant. The nation was still in the Great Depression when he opened on New Year's Day 1938, but Clyde had a way with customers and a knack for barbecue. "He said, 'You need to taste the meat first and not the sauce. The sauce is just the kiss on the meat.'"

Clyde passed away in 1998, and Debbie and her husband, Randy, had made sure to keep cooking the Clyde way. Randy wore a straw hat and wasn't a talker at all, but when I asked about the barbecue and any special ingredients he slipped a sneaky grin and said, "Follow me."

Oh, the countless times I've written about restaurant owners weaving me through narrow corridors to kitchens closeted back in the bowels of buildings and proudly showing me the guts of the operation. *Here goes again*, I thought as Randy started down the long aisle beside the counter. But he suddenly stopped halfway and threw open a door to his left that I hadn't seen before, and I nearly plowed into him like a domino, which would have sent his straw hat flying. "Up here," he said and started clopping up some stairs. I ducked in and shut the door behind me, wondering why he was taking me to the attic.

It wasn't an attic exactly—attics are usually stuffed with dusty trunks, rickety coatracks, and busted high chairs. The second story of Cooper's was empty except for a cooker and a cook, a bald man who was probably in his seventies. He wore a white apron and blue latex gloves and carefully poured a watery brown sauce over a long pan full of chopped barbecue. I was going to ask if he felt lonely working out of sight above the action, but the glint in his eyes and grunt in his throat—"Mm, mm"—told me he was pleased and proud of his work. "Seasoned just the way Clyde done," he said. "People love it."

Randy hoisted the lid on the cooker, which was five times the size of my patio gas grill and where a dozen golden shoulders browned on a metal rack. "It's just slow-cooked all night long, nice and tender and moist."

It seemed an odd place to do the cooking, above the eating. Or maybe it was the perfect place: good ventilation and concentration. Nobody bothered to climb the stairs to bother the cook. "Mm, mm," the man grunted.

As we clopped back down and into the barbecue crowd again, Robert pointed out what I failed to recognize. "Did you see those shoulders?" he asked.

"Sure did," I said.

"How 'bout that sauce?"

"Oh, yeah."

"East meets west," he said, which is where I lost him. "Eastern-style sauce, western-style pig," he added and I finally realized what he meant.

Cooper's cooked the western North Carolina way, only the pig's shoulders and not the whole hog. But its sauce was eastern-style and vinegar-based instead of tomatoey like the west. Here was the dividing line, right here in Raleigh, at Cooper's, which had managed to mingle both styles.

"The best place for barbecue in North Carolina!" bellowed an older gentlemen with a red NC State hat. He told me his age—ninety-three—and said he'd been eating at Cooper's since the place opened seventy-five years ago. "Clyde Cooper was my very good friend," he said. "Cooper's Barbecue is a treasure, an institution!"

I couldn't argue with that—and sure wasn't going to argue with a ninety-three-year-old man who'd seen a lot more history than I had. But I was learning. I'd learned differences between music and barbecue, between old-time and

bluegrass and eastern and western and realized how richly steeped in tradition they are. The music of the mountains isn't just something to hear, and the meat of a hog not merely something to eat. I was coming to understand that both are meaningful symbols rooted in the identities of those who've always called North Carolina home.

"It's the same tables, the chairs, same pictures on the walls," said a man seated in a wooden booth.

"Got the wear and tear that gives it character," said another. "I just hope it stays the same." He laid his palms on the counter as if holding it in place—with good reason.

Cooper's was due to move after seventy-five years in the same location. Debbie told me a developer had bought the building with plans to redo the whole block. She said she hated to go, but there was no choice, and luckily she and Randy had found another building around the corner. "It's going to be okay," she told me, though I don't think she was convinced. "I've prayed about it," she said.

Cooper's had arrived at a tricky turning point. But hadn't it struck the right balance all along, poised itself smartly upon a central geographic axis? Like Debbie had done earlier, I found myself turning 180 degrees and taking in the atmosphere when my eyes landed on the T-shirt with the little piggy's rear end, and I grinned both at the picture and the parallel that popped into mind. Seemed to me Cooper's was the dividing line. The two plump cheeks on either side represented two styles of barbecue. Cooper's Barbecue had dished a harmonious mix of both, upstairs and down, in the same brick building for—75 YEARS! read the circled stamp on the pig's rump. *Bull's-eye*, I thought.

Randy fixed me a full plate, and Sweetie Pie poured me iced tea. I asked her a bunch of questions just to hear her talk. She laughed when she remembered my son eating his whole rack of ribs, and her eyes closed. I laughed, too.

I said good-bye to Sweetie Pie and good luck to Randy and Debbie, and I patted my belly and walked out of Cooper's a contented man, humming a twangy tune.

Nina calls me Condiment Man. I like barbecue with sauce poured all over it, any kind of sauce really. I've even been known to reach for the mayo bottle till Nina says, "Don't you dare." So I go for the Texas Pete instead and add that to my already drowning 'cue.

Of course, a good burger must have mayo, and a hot dog's gotta have mustard—*and* mayo. I save ketchup for french fries and grilled cheese sandwiches and, even then, mix the ketchup with mayonnaise. Ever dip a grilled cheese into a ketchup/mayo mix? Heaven!

I am so thankful to live in North Carolina where family-run restaurants are plentiful, and hot dogs, hamburgers, and barbecue are often specialties of the house. And where the house usually keeps a rack full of condiment bottles at the tables.

MERRITT'S STORE & GRILL

MY SON, SCOUT, LOVES A BACON, LETTUCE, AND TOMATO SANDWICH but without lettuce and tomato, which causes great confusion when he orders one at a restaurant. "I'll have a BLT," Scout says, and the waitress begins to write. "But instead of a BLT can you make it a B, B, and B?" he asks. The waitress stops, lifts her pen and gives him a look. And that's when I jump in.

"What he means," I say, "is that instead of lettuce and tomato, can you just add more bacon? Make it a bacon, bacon, and bacon—a B, B, and B instead of a BLT?" Now she gets it and smiles, not at me but at him. He's eleven and still cute. She puts her pen to her pad again, except the pen doesn't go anywhere and after a moment she lifts it, cups her chin and stares at the ceiling. "B, B, and B," she murmurs. "Wonder how much that costs."

I learned of a little place in Chapel Hill famous for its BLTs. I love BLTs and not just the bacon but the lettuce and tomato, too—and definitely extra mayo. Robert and I aimed west, pulled off I-40 and wound our way to the junction of 54 and 15-501, which seems like a lot of highway numbers for the simple little lunch spot that's located there: Merritt's.

It's a small white building that was once a convenience store and still looks like one, though the pale-blue awnings and patio furniture with colored umbrellas hint at the restaurant inside.

We arrived on a sunny Friday in early summer. People are usually in high spirits on sunny Fridays in early summer. That combination, together with the combination of bacon, lettuce, and tomato, is apt to combine to make one fantastic story. I was excited when I opened the door to Merritt's, and as soon as I did I could feel the energy inside. And I could hear it, too.

"WHOO HOO!" came a shout from somewhere down the aisle to my left. The aisle was packed with people standing in line, waiting to order sandwiches, and the WHOO HOO had everybody laughing and clapping. I realized it must have come from one of the sandwich makers back there, and no wonder he was happy. *Ding, ding!* The cash register was jumping.

The register was at a counter to my right and a man stepped up to pay. He was holding half a dozen sandwiches wrapped in waxed paper, one on top of the other like a tower balanced between his hands. I moved in quickly to interview him.

He told me that he was from California but his daughter lived in Chapel Hill, that he stopped at Merritt's every time he was in town, and that this was the place to buy BLTs. He was stacking up, except his stack seemed as sturdy as a limp slice of bacon, and I let him rest it on the counter and pay. *Ding, ding.* The register rang six times over.

Merritt's had just a few small tables. It was mostly a BLT-to-go type place, and other sandwiches, too. "Pimento cheese on rye!" boomed the voice down the aisle again. "WHOO HOO!"

I noticed several colorful signs, including a long white banner with WELCOME written in pretty blue—painted butterflies flitted above the *W*, *C*, and *M*. The word *Believe*, carved from a wood block into swirly red letters, sat on a shelf. Stenciled on a beam above the aisle was SIMPLY THE BEST FOOD IN TOWN. I also peered at a chalkboard that read MERRITT'S STORE & GRILL SINCE 19 . . . —the last two numbers were smudged but looked like a *2* and a *9*.

"Nineteen twenty-nine is when it started," said a voice over my shoulder. I turned to see a woman in a white blouse and tan jacket, blonde hair tumbling onto her shoulders. "Robin Britt," she said, holding out her hand and introducing herself as the owner.

She invited me to sit and began filling me in on the history of the place. Eben and Ruby Merritt started Merritt's during the Depression, when money was tight and roads were scarce, but the little store became popular with UNC students who'd sit around the pot-bellied stove or lounge on the "liar's bench" and tell stories. Eben and Ruby ran the place for forty-nine years.

Robin said she and her husband started stopping in when they moved to the area in the early '70s. They became such faithful customers that in 1991 they acquired the lease.

"You know, I love my husband a lot," Robin said, "and I would make these huge BLTs for him at home." I pictured a sandwich piled so high it couldn't possibly fit in a mouth. Apparently, Robin's husband had the same idea. He wanted a signature sandwich and began making huge BLTs at the store, his mind set on serving the best BLT in the world. Judging by the popularity of the place, he might have succeeded. "Love is a many-splendored thing, isn't it?" Robin said with a coy smile.

Man, was I ever dying for a Merritt's BLT—with extra mayo—but the line was still long; in fact, it was out the door. "Really, it's the best kept secret of Chapel Hill," said a man nudging my arm. He was pushing forty, which told me this wasn't just a UNC crowd. "You stand here you meet people from everywhere," he said and grinned, and didn't seem at all bothered that he stood in back of the line. It was Friday, he was in high spirits, and the line was moving.

"WHOO HOO!"

I was eager to meet the man with the booming voice and began easing my way to the front, interviewing people along the way. "We love the place," said a man in the middle. "It's worth the drive from Raleigh."

"Food's fantastic," said another. "Everything's really fresh."

I asked a man built like a linebacker what made Merritt's so special, figuring somebody his size would surely say bacon—and maybe even bacon, bacon, and bacon. But he surprised me. "Gotta have a very good tomato," he said in a Lou Rawls baritone, wiggling his meaty fingers for emphasis. "And this guy does not play around with the tomatoes."

I was near the counter now and stood on my tiptoes and tried to catch a glimpse of Mr. WHOO HOO. "Triple on wheat, Lupe!" I heard him shout, pronouncing it "LU-pay," with an accent over the *e*, and I guessed Lupe was the Latino woman on the prep line. I watched her layer lettuce, tomato slices, and bacon onto five open-faced sandwiches, as if making up five miniature beds, though one seemed especially lumpy. The triple on wheat came with triple the bacon, which made for a king-size BLT.

Finally I saw him, the WHOO HOO wonder man. "WHOO HOO!" he belted extra loud and waved me across the counter. "Come on!" he said. "Bring the camera!"

His name was Al, and his face glowed like a newly married man, but I think it was Merritt's he loved: the noise, the crowd, the buzz. "How much bacon do you go through in a day?" I asked.

"Sixty pounds," he said, clearly proud of his pounds.

"Sixty pounds a day, is that a lot?"

"You tell me," he said. "It feels like a lot." He laughed and let rip another howl. "WHOO HOO!"

It was cramped behind the counter, and there was only so much interviewing I could do, but I did talk to Lupe, who was an absolute magician. Al would rattle off six orders at a time, and she'd whip them up, and they'd disappear. "Oh, I love working here when it's busy," she said in broken English, and *her* face glowed, too.

"What'll it be?" Al asked me, and I couldn't resist—although I did resist. How was he going to handle a bacon, bacon, and bacon? But then I figured Lupe would know what to do.

Al hooted when I ordered—the B, B, and B earned two WHOO HOOs. "I'll take it to go," I said when he stopped applauding. *Boy*, I thought, *Scout's gonna be in bacon paradise tonight!* I also ordered a double on white for me.

I thanked Al and Lupe and waved bye to Robin and stepped outside with my hands full and took a last look around. I noted more signs in the parking lot, one on a chalkboard propped against a sawhorse: BLTs UNDER CONSTRUCTION ALL DAY LONG. And another that read WORLD FAMOUS BLTs.

I wished I could have met Robin's husband, but he was busy that day. I would have congratulated him on his signature sandwich, such a simple thing but how people loved it. Though I suspected it wasn't just the sandwich they loved but Merritt's itself—the place, the people, the tradition, all those layers piled into one, a meaningful combination. There was depth to a place like this.

I couldn't wait to peel back the waxed paper on my BLT and dive in. But even more, I wanted to see Scout's face when I handed him his B, B, and B. WHOO HOO!

FLO'S KITCHEN

MY FRIEND KEITH FROM WILSON HAD BEEN FOLLOWING MY TV travels through old-timey restaurants. He'd set foot in many of them himself, being a photographer and columnist for the Wilson newspaper. And by the way, aren't small-town papers great? A photographer can take pictures *and* write stories, and it's comforting to see the same byline on multiple pages because you know that fella has his thumb on the community. Some of my best story ideas come from hometown, homespun dailies and weeklies.

"Oh, you gotta go to Flo's Kitchen," Keith said. We both happened to be covering a civil rights photo exhibition one day in Wilson. The black-and-white freeze frames on the walls around the gallery were powerful and dramatic. "Best biscuits you'll ever eat. I mean, huge." He kept his head down and whispered, trying to look inconspicuous—he was supposed to be admiring the photographs. "Cat head biscuits," he said, or at least I thought that's what he said. The photos kept grabbing my attention.

I leaned close to a picture of black men, arms linked, lining a sidewalk, while mean-faced white men stared back at them across the street, *their* arms folded over their chests. Talk about a serious lack of communication.

"Cat head biscuits," Keith whispered, and I found the image troubling—the one on the wall, too. *Cat head biscuits? Is that what he said?* I turned to look at him, and he popped his head up and grinned—like a Cheshire cat. "Big as a cat's head," he said, and his eyes grew about as big as a cat's head, too.

I grinned back at him and hoped nobody in the gallery noticed. But heck, a big ol' buttery biscuit as big as a cat's head? Keith had planted the image in *my* head without even picking up his camera. Talk about a serious trick of communication. The man was definitely talking my language.

We'd had a run of good food in Wilson—Dick's Hotdog Stand, Parker's, Bill's Barbecue—and I wondered if viewers might think I was biased toward Wilson. But I go where the story is, wherever the food's good, the atmosphere's cozy, and the history and tradition are rich, no bias whatsoever, any diner in any town, several diners in the same town, on one side of the street or the other. But when I arrived at Flo's Kitchen a few weeks later, I didn't expect the first person I met to hail from all the way across the pond.

I think he might have said, "Hello, chap," or "Jolly good morning," or "Top of the day." He definitely did not say, "Heya, good buddy, how ya'll doin'?" He wasn't holding a cat head biscuit either but a camera even bigger than ours.

"BBC," he said in a clipped, stiff-upper-lip accent.

"Good golly," I blurted. "British Broadcasting? What in tarnation you doin' here?"

He told me he and his crew were capturing small-town USA for a new TV series scheduled to air back home. He pronounced the word *scheduled* without the *c* and *d* so that it came out "shejuled." I told him about our own "shejule," hoping he'd warm at my attempt at British brogue, and asked if I could interview him.

"CAT HEAD BISCUITS," KEITH WHISPERED. . . . CAT HEAD BISCUITS? IS THAT WHAT HE SAID? I TURNED TO LOOK AT HIM, AND HE POPPED HIS HEAD UP AND GRINNED—LIKE A CHESHIRE CAT. "BIG AS A CAT'S HEAD," HE SAID, AND HIS EYES GREW ABOUT AS BIG AS A CAT'S HEAD, TOO.

I positioned him in front of Flo's, a little blue-and-white building at the corner of Goldsboro and Downing. "I'm from Glasgow, Scotland," he said and told me more about his assignment. "The friendliness of small-town America and the good food, and this sums it all up." He gestured at the building, and the photo from the gallery suddenly flashed in my head. Talk about two sides of the street—down-home southern and thoroughly European. But the biscuits had apparently bridged the divide—though I did wonder how "cat head biscuits" would translate in the UK.

We traded business cards, and I was struck with the wild thought of the station sending me overseas. *Lots of cozy pubs I could profile over there. Shepherd's pie as big as a cat's head?* But I shook away the idea because, after all, the grass is always greener on the other side of the fence, on the other side of the street, or all the way across the pond.

Flo's was tiny both outside and in. I found the owner squeezed behind the counter with half a dozen other ladies in a cooking space the size of my laundry room. "Didn't this place used to be a gas station?" I asked. Keith had filled me in that day at the gallery.

"It was a gas station, a pool hall. It's one-hundred-twenty years old, this building is," she said with an accent dripped in honey. She told me her name was Linda and pointed to a photo of her mom. "The lady hanging on the wall over there, that's Miss Flo, that's my mother. She died at eighty and was still making biscuits down here when she died."

Miss Flo wore a bright pastel shirt in the picture and beamed at the camera. She held a miniature birthday cake in her hands, big enough to handle only eight candles instead of eighty. "Mama said it's bigger than a cat's head." Linda meant the biscuits, not the cake. "We put the cheese in the biscuit, hoop cheese," she said and demonstrated with her hands, like she was plopping a hunk of hoop in her palm, a thick wedge. "Big ol' big biscuit!" she exclaimed and spread her hands wide.

It tickled me listening to Linda's southern accent. She rang the register and handed a man his change. "Thank you, shug," she said and peeked at me over his shoulder and smiled. "Everybody's a 'shug' here or a 'honey' or 'sweetie.'" She turned back to him. "Don't be a stranger, hon."

The woman working the drive-through window was the same. "Cat head, here you go, sweetie," she said, leaning out the window slot with a bag and handing it to a man in a pickup. She straightened and poked her head back in. "Most of these people come every day," she told me, grabbed another bag and leaned out the window again. "Here you go, shug!"

I poked my own head halfway out and saw cars wrapped around the building and figured it would be good to interview some of the folks waiting in line. I slipped outside and tapped the first window I came to, and when it rolled down a man the size of Paul Bunyan stared back at me. "Best restaurant in the South!" he boomed when I asked, and I thanked him—but I did not call him "sweetie."

"The food is just good homemade, like straight from the kitchen," said a woman in a rusty four-door, bouncing in her seat as she described the scrumptious biscuits. I would have asked her more but she punched the gas, and her car lurched forward. The line was moving.

I wasn't the only one scampering around, tapping on windows. A skinny lady with pen and pad raced from car to car, scribbling orders. No wonder she was so thin; the line looked a mile long. I stopped her long enough to clip on a mic, and from then on it was all "sugar" and "honey." "Chitlin biscuit and an egg, honey? All righty, shug. See you later, sweetie."

Listening to all those orders had me craving a cat head. Even a chitlin biscuit sounded tempting, and I jumped back inside.

"Oh, Lord, they're huge!" howled a man at a booth. "Can't eat more than one! Come to Flo's!" he whooped and slapped the table.

We'd skipped Bojangles' on the drive over, and it was near torture being at Flo's on an empty stomach, too busy to eat a biscuit and watching people eating biscuits, which, by the way, looked soft and fluffy with trickles of steam rising over golden domes. I licked my lips and stepped to the counter, ready to place my order when a pat on my back stopped me.

It was my buddy Keith, who'd swung by to see how I was making out. He grinned. "Didn't I tell you?" he said and waved a hand at the room, and when I looked around, the picture I'd seen at the photo gallery came creeping back again. Flo's was just the opposite of that intense street scene. Black and white folks sat elbow to elbow and, granted, there *was* a lack of communication but only because everybody's mouth was full. *Gosh*, I thought, *if only Flo's had been alongside that other street in the 1960s. Bet some warm cat head biscuits would have softened the tension.*

Keith ordered from Linda, and we sat down, and he folded his hands and propped them beneath his chin. "So you wanna know about Flo's?" he said, looking like the Flo's expert he was.

"Well, no," I told him. "I want to know about *eating* at Flo's." I didn't have to wait long for my answer. A waitress came around with Keith's plate, though I couldn't see the plate for the size of the biscuit.

"I usually get the tenderloin," he said, using both hands to pick it up. "This biscuit's the size of three biscuits most places." He bounced it in his hands to show how heavy it was and then put it in his mouth and rolled his eyes in ecstasy. Talk about communicating—without uttering a word.

I finally placed my own order—a bacon, egg, and cheese cat head. "Here you go, hon," the waitress said, and like Keith I used both hands to scoop it up. But as hungry as I was, I didn't take a bite right away. Instead, I admired it a moment. The biscuit was as big as a fist but soft as a pillow. When I at last opened wide I noticed everybody watching me, the TV reporter trying his first Flo's biscuit. The man who'd whooped and laughed earlier was now gripping the corner of the table and leaning on the edge of his chair. I shut my eyes and bit in.

And what a biscuit it was—light, fluffy, warm, bacon, egg, and cheese. "Mmm, mmm," I murmured, which was communication enough. The man slapped the table and laughed loud and hard. "Oh, yeah, yeah!"

And me? I grinned like a Cheshire cat.

BRITT'S DONUTS
(AND THE VENUS FLYTRAP)

I'D HEARD ABOUT A LITTLE DONUT SHOP ALONG THE BOARDWALK at Carolina Beach that had stood for more than seventy years and was a cherished landmark. Go to the beach, stop at Britt's—just part of the routine.

The place sounded fun, except that Britt's made only glazed donuts and no other kind. *What's so hard about a jelly donut?* I thought. Jelly's my favorite. *Or shoot, I'd even settle for the old-fashioned cake kind with a hot cup of coffee.*

It was midsummer and I sat at my desk feeling both hungry and pale. I peered over my cubicle at the newshounds in scratchy suits and thought, *What am I waiting for? A beach trip it is! And, okay, a glazed donut, too.*

But before coasting to the coast I pulled my East folder, looking for other possible stories in New Hanover County, and I found a particularly good one that also had to do with eating—sort of.

To the beach we went, but not the beach-beach with the boardwalk and Britt's. Instead, we stopped first at Carolina Beach State Park, a quiet retreat popular with walkers and joggers. And well-known for another type of trail.

I meandered along the shady path, cutting my eyes left and right but seeing nothing except leafy trees and pine needles. I began to think I'd taken a wrong turn when Robert cried, "There they are!" and pointed to the ground. "Tons of 'em."

I squinted and bent close to one. "That?"

"That's it," he said "That's a Venus flytrap."

I'd seen the movie *Little Shop of Horrors*, which featured a man-eating monster plant with wild gangly limbs and a huge mouth. I knew the movie exaggerated, but here I was on the famous Venus flytrap trail, and the peewee pod at my feet was barely bigger than a half dollar. It looked like a green palm-size pouch with its zipper open. I watched a bug crawl across the zipper's teeth, then veer

downhill into the mouth of the pouch. It dawdled around down there until, *WHAM!* The mouth snapped shut and trapped the bug.

Jeez, I thought and reared back. For such a puny plant it sure packed a punch. The poor bugger inside was history.

Robert is not a walker or jogger but that day he was a sprinter. He'd left his camera in the car and ran to fetch it before another bug made a boneheaded move. He was eager to capture as many victims as he could.

But it never fails: Bugs, gnats, and flies swarm when you don't want them and disappear when you do. I crouched by one of the plants and willed another insect, just one teeny-tiny pest, to crawl into the trap, a sacrifice for the sake of our camera. But after ten minutes my legs began to cramp, and I stood and lurched for the nearest tree to keep from falling over.

And that's when the park ranger showed up who may have been a tree hugger, too. I'd never seen sideburns as long as his. They stretched almost to the corners of his mouth. He looked like a '70s hippie, except for his khaki uniform and green Smokey-the-Bear hat.

"Only found in this part of the world, nowhere else," he said, and for a moment I thought he meant his sideburns. "Kinda like a mousetrap. Inside that leaf are three trigger hairs, and when an insect crawls inside, it hits those hairs and the leaf slaps shut."

"Must be like walking through a minefield?" I said. He nodded, nearly whacking my nose with the brim of his hat. "But what do you mean the Venus flytrap is only found in this part of the world?"

"It grows naturally within a seventy-mile radius of Wilmington, North Carolina, and nowhere else," he said. "We really don't know why they're found here, but it's the park's claim to fame. We get visitors from all over the world. 'Course, they come looking for Seymour from the *Little Shop of Horrors* if they've never seen one before." I didn't tell him I'd been expecting Seymour, too, who in the movie devours an unsuspecting businessman in one gulp.

Robert and I settled for bugs and flies, and we lingered long enough to witness several of them finally trip the triggers, their fate an open-and-shut case. The plants were impressive, and I knew we had a good story. And I also realized something else: I was ravenous.

The Carolina Beach boardwalk was crowded with families in flip-flops and tanned skinny women in bright bikinis. I soaked up the atmosphere and imagined my colleagues back at the station huddled at their computers beneath the buzz of florescent lights, nibbling on stale peanut-butter Nabs. Those poor buggers were trapped, too, zipped in the mouth of the TV news beast.

I spotted a building near the boardwalk arcade with a blue-and-white awning and a sign on the front: BRITT'S DONUT SHOP SINCE 1939. After a morning spent with Venus flytraps, I was glad to see the place didn't have a door but just a wide-open entryway: Stroll in, pull up a stool, order, and enjoy. I loved the laid-back atmosphere, the whirring ceiling fans, and sugary smells. And the bikini-clad women.

"Every time you get them they're soft and light and airy," said a young mom in a pink tank top holding her fidgety toddler who was definitely *not* light and airy. His cheeks puffed out like a blowfish, one donut in his mouth and another pinched between his fingers.

"I been driving since nine fifteen this morning for these donuts," said a man with flip-up sunglasses. He stood at the cash register with bills in his hand and four bags on the counter. It was well past noon.

The counter was long and full of elbows, and I watched people savor their donuts. "I love them!" said a blonde little girl who'd probably collected enough tooth-fairy money to buy a dozen. She was missing all but two fangs on either side of her top row. "I like the taste," she said with a lisp.

I met owner Bobby Nivens. He had wispy gray hair and a salt-and-pepper mustache and said he'd worked at Britt's as a teenager and then bought it from Mr. Britt in 1974. He told me he enjoyed the schedule—open day and night from Memorial Day to Labor Day but closed the rest of the year.

We'd caught Bobby at busy peak season, but I think the atmosphere energized him, all those happy people with sand in their hair and sugar in their veins.

"A GLAZED DONUT, THAT'S ALL WE'VE EVER MADE," SAID BOBBY. "TENDER LOVING CARE. AND WE HAVE A GOOD RECIPE." HE SAID IT WAS A SECRET RECIPE, BUT SUGAR WAS OBVIOUSLY THE OVERRIDING INGREDIENT—SO OVERRIDING THAT AFTER BREATHING IN THE GOOPY FUMES I WAS READY TO STAND UNDER THE CEILING FANS AGAIN.

He showed me to the kitchen in back where I watched a man load fifteen donuts on a long stick and dunk the dowel into a vat of white goop. Then he pulled out the stick and set it on hooks, which allowed the excess glaze to drip into the trough below.

"A glazed donut, that's all we've ever made," said Bobby. "Tender loving care. And we have a good recipe." He said it was a secret recipe, but sugar was obviously the overriding ingredient—so overriding that after breathing in the goopy fumes I was ready to stand under the ceiling fans again.

When I slipped back out to the shop I recognized the man just walking in, unmistakable with his jet-black eyebrows and Carolina-blue Polo. It was Dick Baddour, UNC's athletic director. He was with his family, and I wasn't sure how he'd feel about a reporter bothering him for an interview at the beach. So I walked up to his wife instead.

She beamed and put a hand over her heart as if to say, *Me? You want to interview me?* We chatted a minute, and she never stopped smiling, and she tugged her husband's arm and he smiled, too, and introduced his grandsons and said, "Why don't you interview us all?" I could have hugged him.

I positioned the four of them sitting together on stools, and what a nice family photo it was—Dick in his blue shirt, his wife in a sundress, and the boys looking tanned and healthy. "I've been coming to Britt's for sixty years," Dick said and told me he owned a house at Carolina Beach. "We love it here," he said.

"You can sit and watch them make the donuts," added his wife. "They can't be any fresher."

Fresh and only one kind and no doors at all, sweet and simple. I watched Dick Baddour, in his sixtieth year of visiting Britt's, brush away crumbs and smile at his wife and grandsons. I could have hugged them all.

Which makes it all so sad when I think of the Baddours that day. I didn't know it then—none of us did—but their world would soon become awfully complicated. News broke of a major scandal at UNC involving athletes and agents and academic fraud. Football players had accepted money and gifts and registered for classes that never met. One scandal erupted into another, and in the end the university fired its head football coach, and the chancellor himself resigned. And so did Dick Baddour. He'd apparently been unaware of the danger, but crept too close to the hot spot and brushed against the triggers. The door slammed shut on his UNC career.

I thanked the Baddours, who seemed to get a kick out of being interviewed and enjoyed being together. They eventually rose from their stools, and I watched them walk out of Britt's into the busy world outside. I never saw Dick again, except in the newspapers.

"You can't have a bad day if you're working in a donut shop," said the clerk behind the counter, and she threw back her head and laughed. And then she plucked a hot one straight from the dunking vat and handed it to me.

A woman nearby saw me eyeing it before I ate it. "Sugary sweet," she said with a reassuring nod. I chomped half, and she was right. It even rivaled a jelly donut.

The woman smiled, probably because of the glaze on my nose, but she was obviously delighted at witnessing a newbie sample his first Britt's donut. And she, in turn, delighted me because *her* bite, her next *sound* bite, summed up my whole story. "It's just simple," she said.

SHERRY'S BAKERY
(AND THE SPLIT BRITCHES)

WHEN I THINK OF SHERRY'S BAKERY I ALSO THINK OF JORDAN'S Jewelry Store. They're a block from each other in downtown Dunn, and though I visited them on separate occasions, in my mind they're linked like needle and thread.

I was in Harnett County one day in early spring, and as Robert and I drove into downtown Dunn, I thought of our trip to Sherry's Bakery a few months earlier. "The Sweetest Smelling Corner in Town" is the bakery's motto, and it sure is sweet smelling, full of sugary goodies. I almost told Robert to hang a right on North Wilson, but if we stopped for a bite at Sherry's I knew we'd be there for an hour eating and talking, and we were due at the little jewelry shop on Broad.

Jordan's was about to celebrate its 125th anniversary, and when I walked in and greeted the two ladies behind the counter, they told me they were pretty sure it was the oldest jewelry store in the state.

I'm reluctant to call them little old ladies, but I don't think they'd mind. Joyce was the short, perky one who spoke right up when I asked her age. "Seventy-nine," she said. "Been here sixty-one years. I started working for Mr. Jordan when I was in high school." She bought the store from Mr. Jordan in 1954, and I admired both her dedication and her hairdo, which glowed with a reddish tint.

The other woman was Joyce's older sister, whom Joyce had recruited for the store eighteen years earlier. "I love it," said Virginia, whose dark hair sat high and fluffy.

"Do you two get along?" I asked.

"Most of the time," said Joyce.

"Most of the time," said Virginia.

The two of them were great on camera, and as I joked with Virginia and Joyce I bounced a bit on my toes, knowing I had a winner. Maybe it was the bouncing that did it or the jumble of keys in my pocket, but as I chatted away and rested a hand on my hip for better bouncing balance, I realized one side of my pants had split wide open. Oh my gosh, my boxers were hanging out! Good thing I wasn't wearing the ones with little penguins.

We had two more stories to shoot in Harnett County that day and maybe a bite at Sherry's Bakery, and what in the world was I going to do? I think Virginia and Joyce knew something was wrong because my face must have turned as white as my thigh; my legs hadn't seen the summer sun in months.

The cat was out of the bag, and my boxers were out of my pants, and Virginia and Joyce were bent over laughing. "The Tar Heel Traveler splits his britches. Now that's a story!" they cackled, and then I must have looked like I'd been in the sun too long. I felt my face turn as red as a beet.

Joyce sputtered something about needle and thread, and Virginia disappeared in the back and returned with a small box. She sat down and grabbed my shredded pants but kept giggling and jiggling the needle, which snaked awfully close to my bare flesh. "Oh, Lord, don't want to prick the Tar Heel Traveler's nekked leg," she said. I wasn't much help. My leg shook because I was giggling, too.

After many false starts and near misses the needle found its groove, and so what if my corduroys were blue and the thread brown? At least my boxers were safely tucked inside. And maybe my shirttail, too. "Hope I didn't sew it to your pants," Virginia said.

"The Tar Heel Traveler's shirt sewn to his britches!" Joyce howled, and the two of them got to laughing all over again.

I felt like I'd known Virginia and Joyce for years. We became very close, you might say, and the two of them gave me a great big hug. Before leaving, I checked the brass clock on the shelf and thought I might just have time to sneak by Sherry's Bakery before the next shoot—although I did wonder about eating too many donuts and busting the thread.

———

Sherry's Bakery is both a bakery and restaurant that fit together like thimble and finger. The bakery is on one side, the restaurant on the other and the smells of donuts and pastries mingle with bacon and eggs. It's a big place with lots of tables and booths, and people eat or just sit and talk and drink coffee. Maybe it's the caffeine and sugar that create such a lively atmosphere. I gazed through the glass display case filled with row upon row of cookies, cakes, and pies.

Freddie Williford caught me drooling and introduced himself. He was the eighty-something-year-old owner but moved with a spring in his step. "C'mon," he said, like a young man in a hurry.

He led me through the Employees Only section to a back room twenty times the size of my kitchen with refrigerators and ovens ten times the size of my own. *My wife would love this*, I thought.

THUD! I jumped at the noise and looked around, thinking sugar must have eaten away an axle and flung a ball bearing against the wall. *THUD!* Two ball bearings?

SHERRY'S BAKERY IS BOTH A BAKERY AND RESTAURANT THAT FIT TOGETHER LIKE THIMBLE AND FINGER. THE BAKERY IS ON ONE SIDE, THE RESTAURANT ON THE OTHER, AND THE SMELLS OF DONUTS AND PASTRIES MINGLE WITH BACON AND EGGS. IT'S A BIG PLACE WITH LOTS OF TABLES AND BOOTHS, AND PEOPLE EAT OR JUST SIT AND TALK AND DRINK COFFEE.

My eyes landed on a wiry man with a hairnet heaving donuts into a vat of chocolate, like a pitcher hurling strikes into a catcher's mitt. *THUD!* But he was careful with his throws—no knuckleballs for him. The donuts landed flat on one side for an even coating. The man was good. I stood nearby, and yet my shirt avoided the spray. Thankfully, no hits for me. *THUD!* Another strike.

"Good, good, good, good!" Freddie said, punching each word and waving his arms over a loaded tray. "Honey buns, chocolate honey buns, chocolate-nut honey buns, and cream-filled oatmeal cookies." He held up one of the cookies like a prized medallion. "People come here from all over everywhere for our oatmeal cookies."

Freddie was just getting started. He picked up what looked like an oversize hot dog roll with cream in place of the dog and gooped in chocolate instead of ketchup. "What we call a Long John," he said, aiming it at me. "Look, freshness is the key to success in a bakery. If it's not fresh, throw it out." I sure hoped he wasn't going to throw out the Long John. I would have eaten it if it was three days old. And besides, it made for a good pointing stick.

Freddie told me he'd been driving a bread truck when he bought the bakery in 1967. "This is going on forty-five years."

"You still enjoy it?"

"Yes, sir," he said and gripped both sides of the table as if delivering an impassioned speech. "Love it to death. Fine people. That's what I love about it is the people."

The kitchen sweets made great video, but the mention of people made me realize I needed to interview some. Freddie waved the Long John. "Go ahead, mingle," he said.

I hustled to the restaurant section and picked a table full of gray-haired coffee drinkers, thinking all that caffeine might be good for some wisecracks.

"We call this the Wisdom Club," said a man in a yellow sweater. "It only takes one vote to get in, and you can vote for yourself." I knew right away I'd chosen the right group.

"What do we talk about?" said another man when I asked. "Well, when there's no women around we talk about the women."

"Philosophizing and passing on wisdom and stuff," said a third fellow to the head-nodding consensus of the table.

I asked about their age. "Seventy-nine," cried one, rapping his cup against the table top, but then he shook his head. "'Scuse me," he muttered. "I'm seventy-eight." He grinned and slouched and turned red in the face, but his buddy came to his rescue.

"I'm glad to be here at any age!" he said, which drew a round of laughs.

I also interviewed some women, one who said she'd been coming to Sherry's since she was eight years old and now brought her grandchildren. Another grandma told me her wedding cake had come from Sherry's, and I marveled at her years of loyalty. I also wondered who Sherry was.

I posed the question to Freddie, who said the bakery was originally called Dunn Right. *Catchy*, I thought. But Freddie and his wife, Mary, had a six-year-old daughter at the time and decided to name it after her. "It's a family bakery," Mary said, and so Sherry's it was. *Well, that's pretty catchy, too.*

Mary was quite a bit shorter than Freddie, but they made a great picture standing side by side with an arm around each other. "Even the customers are like family," she said.

Many of those customers hugged me before I left, just as Virginia and Joyce had hugged me back at the jewelry store. They were both hugging kinds of places, the people gracious and good-hearted.

But that's how it is in this rural corner of North Carolina, on the sweetest-smelling corner in town or in the oldest jewelry store in the state. Walk in a stranger, leave as a friend. In Harnett County, that's the common thread.

Freddie and Mary presented me with a big box to take home. I tried to tell them no, that I was going to get fat and bust a seam, but they insisted. And truth be told, I hoped they'd packed a Long John inside and maybe a couple of their famous oatmeal cookies. I was sure going to enjoy them. And when I did, I'd remember not to wear my boxers with the little penguins—just in case.

YUM YUM

MY FAVORITE TIME OF YEAR IS THE FIRST WEEK OF JUNE. AS A KID it was always the last week of school before summer break. Vacation was days away, and everybody in class was excited, even the teachers. I loved the anticipation. And we didn't do much work that last week of school anyway.

June is also my favorite time to shoot stories. The weather is good, people are happy, the trees are green and flowers in bloom, and the stories just seem easier to gather. A June day writing and editing is a wasted day. The month is meant for getting out, riding with the windows down, stopping to chat and shoot. The more stories the merrier.

We wound through UNC-Greensboro that first Thursday in June and I felt—discombobulated. Our navigation system was taking us down no-name streets, and I was growing impatient, even though I'd become attached to the pleasant-sounding woman who ordered us to turn left and right and left again. She spoke with supreme confidence, but I was thinking she had to be confused. *Your destination is ahead on the right*, she said with perfect enunciation, but that meant our destination was the side of a nondescript building when we'd been looking for a popular local landmark.

Robert rolled forward, and I spotted a sign we might be in the right place after all: a long white limousine parked at the curb. "This has gotta be it," I told Robert.

"Must be," he said.

Your guidance is now complete, the woman said.

Our destination was Yum Yum Better Ice Cream, a humble little building at the edge of a parking lot. I learned the limo had dropped off a pile of fifth graders who'd just graduated from elementary school, and before long they spilled out of Yum Yum licking their cones, boys in Lacoste shirts and Bermuda shorts, ponytailed girls in matching pink-and-blue T-shirts with big white stars on the collars and sleeves. They sat on the brick wall in front of the store, a long line of swinging Top-Siders and sandals, and I thought, *Boy, if Norman Rockwell were here . . .* This was hometown America and more, one flavorful scoop of the South.

I felt like a kid again myself, though not that I particularly wanted an ice cream cone. It was hot that day, and the happy graduates were unanimously licking their wrists and arms. A mom hurried down the line passing out napkins, which didn't do a thing but create more of a sticky mess. I looked over at Robert, who was grinning and shooting and eating up the scene playing through his viewfinder. I asked him for the car keys so I could run grab my sunscreen. I figured we'd be here awhile. Then again, the way the ice cream was melting, maybe not.

"It's really good," slurped a redheaded boy when I returned, and I probably should have offered *him* my sunscreen.

"You ready for middle school?" I asked.

"Ready," he said, tongue working furiously. I love it when my interview subjects forget about the camera and act naturally, but what I really wanted to do was grab the cone, dump it in a paper cup, and snatch him some Wet Ones. "It's really big," he said, and I wasn't sure if he meant the ice cream or the move up to sixth grade.

I hadn't planned on meeting freckly-faced eleven-year-olds fresh from their graduation assembly; it just happened that way, but as a reporter those finds are like gems that make people smile, even if they might want to reach through the TV and wipe chocolate drips off the boys' alligator shirts. We rolled on that cone-licking scene till the very last lick.

Orange chairs lined the front of Yum Yum, plastic bucket seats bolted to iron poles but swiveling loosey-goosey-like. Their art-deco color and shape made me think of the 1970s. I watched young and old slurp strawberry and chocolate chip, tap their shoes to the concrete, and gently spin left and right, no one in a hurry at all. The scene reminded me of the '70s, too.

> FIFTH GRADERS . . . SPILLED OUT OF YUM YUM LICKING THEIR CONES, BOYS IN LACOSTE SHIRTS AND BERMUDA SHORTS, PONYTAILED GIRLS IN MATCHING PINK-AND-BLUE T-SHIRTS. . . . THEY SAT ON THE BRICK WALL IN FRONT OF THE STORE, A LONG LINE OF SWINGING TOP-SIDERS AND SANDALS. . . . BOY, IF NORMAN ROCKWELL WERE HERE . . . THIS WAS HOMETOWN AMERICA AND MORE, ONE FLAVORFUL SCOOP OF THE SOUTH.

But the orange seats must have been a late addition because Yum Yum started way back in 1906. "Well Grandpa, he loved ice cream," said Clint, the store's fair-skinned VP. His grandpa was W. B. and first sold ice cream from a horse and wagon. "One of Grandpa's first flavors was called Yum Yum," Clint said.

He walked me inside and not a moment too soon. We'd both been squinting, and I'm sure the VP wasn't wearing SP.

There was nothing fancy about Yum Yum: a square room, bare floor, and bare walls, except for framed photos and newspaper clippings hanging here and there. Wooden booths lined the left wall and filled the middle, and to the right stretched the ice-cream counter with half a dozen staffers digging into buckets and piling huge helpings onto funnel cones. Scooping ice cream might have been better than pumping iron; it took strength to pry it loose, and the crew was certainly getting plenty of reps. Customers leaned against the counter from one end to the other, anticipating that first luscious lick.

I squeezed past the line and followed Clint through a narrow doorway into a much darker room with all the sounds of a factory. I heard *thunks, bangs,* and *buzzes,* but when my eyes adjusted, it wasn't pistons and steel I noticed but a girl with a baseball cap pulled low and a cute-as-a-button smile. I wondered if she was a UNC-G student, or maybe a recent grad. "Fourth-generation ice-cream maker," Clint said and introduced his niece, who wiped her hands on her shirt and stuck one out for a shake.

She'd been filling a long tin barrel with soft-serve, and she turned to re-center it beneath one of the contraptions. When she pulled the lever, a rich, creamy swirl began curling into the container. "It's coffee ice cream," she said. "And it's really awesome." Her smile had me melting, and so did the flavor. I love coffee ice cream.

"We're the only small company in North Carolina that still makes ice cream from scratch," Clint said. He'd struck me as quiet but raised his voice over the racket—and maybe puffed out his chest a little, too; the creases in his apron disappeared. If he was camera shy, I think he was over it. "The store's been in my family for more than a hundred years," he said and led me back through the doorway and pointed to the photos and clippings on the wall.

"This is the original store that was built in 1922," he said. The building in the picture was solid brick with something akin to a turret rising from the center. It looked like a castle. But UNC-G was king. When the university expanded, Yum Yum had to move across the street. *Maybe that's why the navigation woman was so confused*, I thought.

I told Clint his guidance was now complete, thanked him for the tour, and began working my way from booth to booth.

"I remember the days when there were bumper stickers that said, SAVE YUM YUM, SELL UNC-G," a man told me and chuckled. Of course, it was all tongue and cheek; the neighbors were practically partners. One institution fed the other, the two as intertwined as a chocolate-and-vanilla swirl.

People told me they'd been coming to Yum Yum for years. "Since I was a teenager," said one lady who was not a *young* lady. "But if I tell you too much, I'll be telling you my age!"

One man held up his shake for the camera. "It's good," he said. "So thick I can hardly get it through the straw."

A little girl showed me her empty dish of ice cream and half-eaten hot dog and said they were her two favorite foods. "Nowhere else can you get a hot dog like a Yum Yum hot dog," Mom said. But at this table dessert apparently came first.

I ordered a coffee cone before I left, although being on TV makes me a bit mindful of sticking my tongue out in public. I turned to the window as if admiring the day and began biting my way through a scoop.

I spotted the fifth-grade graduates gathering again at the curb. They must have lingered around and had seconds since much of their firsts ended up on their clothes. I signaled to Robert, and we scrambled out and videotaped them piling into the limousine, bouncing on the seats and cranking up the stereo.

Soon the doors closed and the limo pulled onto the road, and I knew that was our closing shot. They were kids with bellies full of ice cream and a whole summer stretched in front of them, and then it was on to middle school. But best not to think about that right now. Now was fun and innocence and Norman Rockwell and a limo ride home. And ice cream dripping all over my fingers and wrist.

I'd forgotten about my cone, and stood and licked, and suddenly didn't care who saw me. And it was fun feeling like a kid again, remembering just how much I love the first week of June, all those early Junes of my youth—before my youth slipped away.

I watched the limousine disappear into the distance and thought, *Man, I envy those kids.*

BESSIE

I WAS BUSY THE SPRING DAY I SENT ROBERT SOUTH TO SAMPSON
County to shoot a flowering dogwood tree. Experts had certified it as the largest
dogwood in the country, 31-feet tall with a trunk 114 inches around. Experts aren't
sure of its age but determined it was already a mature tree in 1864. I'd seen the
dogwood back in February and interviewed a woman who told me all about it, but
an ugly tangle of bare branches beneath a black sky did not make a pretty picture.

Now it was four months later, and I looked for another story Robert could
shoot on his return trip to the tree, now in bloom, while I stayed behind to
write. I opened my Sampson County file and discovered Bessie.

The e-mail came from her employer, who said Bessie was a cherished part of
the family ice-cream shop. It went on about how dependable she was and that
she'd been serving up delicious soft-serve for fifty-eight years. "Ever since we
opened," said the note.

Fifty-eight years. Wow. I wondered if Sampson County not only had the country's largest dogwood tree but also the longest ice-cream server. *Must be one special lady*, I thought, and my eyes skipped to the next line:

She's made with tractor parts.

"What?!" I blurted, and the anchorwoman at the opposite desk peered at
me over our cubicles.

"Sorry," I told her and kept reading. I learned Bessie the beloved ice-cream
server was packed with nuts and bolts: *We have confirmed she is the oldest ice-cream
machine in southeastern North America*, read the note.

Well, it certainly was an ice-cream story with a twist, I thought, and imagined a towering chocolate-coffee swirl. *Mmmm.*

I searched the e-mail for her employer, found it, and blurted another,
"What?!" and this time the anchorwoman *glared* at me over the cubicles. I'd

assumed Bessie belonged to a quaint mom-and-pop shop, and what a cute story that would be. But Bessie's owner was Dairy Queen.

Fast food chains line the thoroughfares of America, but the Tar Heel Traveler is all about the back roads of North Carolina. I do love a Bojangles' biscuit and enjoy McDonald's coffee and have always admired Wendy's founder Dave Thomas, but it's not likely I'd do a story on any of them. Besides, I'd probably have to call the corporate office for permission and send a complete list of interview questions, and maybe somebody would get back to me in a month after taking the request under advisement.

But Bessie seemed too good to pass up. The Dairy Queen was in Clinton, and I picked up the phone. "Sure," the lady on the line said with a hop and a skip in her voice, and relief washed through me like a root-beer float on a steamy day. "Come on down," she said full of folksy friendliness—and she did not ask me to call the corporate office.

I hung up and cried, "Yes!"—luckily, the anchorwoman had left her desk. I had another one for the stockpile. Robert would stop by Dairy Queen on the way to the dogwood and bring back the story for me to write. I just hoped the lady with the hop and a skip wouldn't be disappointed. Robert would interview her for sure, but she wasn't the one I really wanted.

I wanted Bessie.

Robert doesn't shoot many stories on his own—I like to be there—but sometimes the workload demands it. On his drive back from Clinton he sent me a text full of exclamation marks, and I figured the Dairy Queen piece had either gone well or he'd loaded up on too much sugar.

I screened the video when he came in the door, and there was Bessie, lovely boxy Bessie—clunky, clanky, and all shiny and metal. "Fifty-eight years old and yet she's like a spry young teenager," said a DQ server named Billy, who was barely older than a teenager himself. He lifted the lid off Bessie, and my headphones rattled with the vibration of her inner workings; the audio levels on the tape machine licked at the red zone, but I watched with fascination. She was built with pistons that spun and an iron wheel that whirled. A thick rubber belt went round and round. Billy listed all the tractor parts and pointed at her stumpy legs. "They're actually bolted five feet into the ground and held in with concrete."

I learned it was Billy's grandparents who'd opened the store, fast food entrepreneurs in the days before fast food. They took a chance on their DQ franchise in small-town Clinton, and the store had become a local landmark. "Same ice cream recipes they used back in 1953 are still used here today, not to mention some of the original machinery," Billy said and gave Bessie a pat.

Robert shot Bessie at work pumping ice cream, which plopped from a tube into the cones that Billy and his brother Christian held underneath. "Hot day, you've been at the pool, been running around, nothing better than ice cream," Christian said. He swiveled the cone and made a perfect vanilla curl at the top. I heard Robert ask how many cones Bessie had served over fifty-eight years. "Definitely millions," Christian said.

Billy grabbed Robert's attention again and walked over to the windows and pointed up, and when Robert zoomed in I saw scratches zigzagging all over the metal frames. The camera zoomed tighter, and I realized the scratches spelled names: Aaron, Kristina, Carolyn, David. "Employees would engrave their names into the windows," Billy said. "See, everybody's name all the way back to the late '50s." *Definitely not your corporate DQ*, I thought and smiled at those ragged marks. To me they were a thing of beauty.

> THERE WAS BESSIE, LOVELY BOXY BESSIE—CLUNKY, CLANKY, AND ALL SHINY AND METAL. "FIFTY-EIGHT YEARS OLD AND YET SHE'S LIKE A SPRY YOUNG TEENAGER."

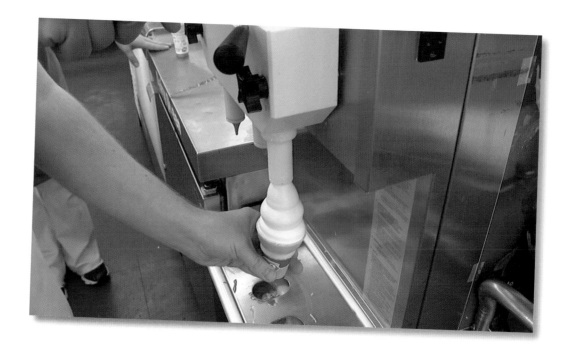

And so were all those shots of kids and families. Robert captured one little girl at the take-out window who couldn't stop giggling, and I knew I'd tuck those funny giggles into my story.

He also interviewed the owner, and Tamara was as friendly on camera as she'd been on the phone. She was Billy and Christian's mom; the Dairy Queen was a family operation. "I have people come up here all the time who say, 'Oh, my grandfather brought me here when I was a child, and now I'm doing this for my grandkids.'" I realized the hop and skip in her voice was pride and joy.

What a story I had and what a surprise. I'd thought the Dairy Queen was just another cog in a corporate machine. But the machine was the best part, that and all those close-ups of kids licking their swirly ice cream, fresh from Bessie the ice-cream machine.

Billy held a cone beneath the tube, pulled the lever, and soon had a perfect pyramid. "We're gonna keep doing things the exact same way we've done for fifty-eight years," he said and smiled for the camera. And with his other hand he gave Bessie a gentle pat.

SUNNI SKY'S

I STUMBLED ACROSS A TV STORY ONLINE ABOUT AN ICE-CREAM store in Angier, south of Raleigh. The camera shot hovered over a barrel of ice cream the color of clay, a sort of faded red, like what you might find at a North Carolina construction site. The camera zoomed in, and I spotted something fat and green half buried in the gook. Red ones, too. *Gotta be gummy worms*, I told myself.

The camera cut away to a reporter I recognized from a competing station. I liked Frank, and he sure seemed to be having a good time, leaning back in a rocking chair with a crowd around him, yapping with the anchorman and woman. He'd rolled up his shirtsleeves and hadn't even bothered to hide his mic cord, which draped halfway over his shoulder.

The anchors said something about trying the ice cream, and the crowd leaned in as Frank dipped a plastic spoon into a bowl of the red clay. "Here goes," he said and gave the folks back home a wide toothy grin.

He scraped a pea-size sample onto his tongue, and nobody moved. Even the camera stayed steady, frozen on Frank. Nobody spoke—you could have heard a gummy worm drop. But then came a sound, a grunt, and the crowd bent closer because it came from Frank. And what was going on with Frank's pupils? They looked like they might spring from his head and bop the lens. And Frank's face? It burned fire-engine red, and sweat popped out on his cheeks and nose. He gasped for air and pounded his chest and shook all over, yet somehow the mic cord still clung to his shoulder. "Water, water!" he blurted, and the circle of spectators hooted and clapped. "Ughhh!" he cried and lurched for a plastic water bottle, threw back his head, and guzzled, while half the bottle ran down his chin, which brought more laughs and knee slaps. The anchors tried to ask Frank a question, but all they got was, "Ughhh!"

"Oh, brother," I murmured. The spectacle was so over the top it was funny, bad funny. I had to hand it to ol' Frank, he even had *me* chuckling.

So the gummy worms were actually hot peppers, and the ice cream was called Cold Sweat. Frank brushed away his own sweat, gave his chest another pound, whirled a sheet of paper at the camera and explained in a raspy voice that it was a waiver form. You had to sign a waiver before attempting the spicy ice cream. He shook his head like he'd been punched in the nose and reminded me of a jowl-jiggling, splotchy-faced Richard Nixon. "Water," he croaked again. And the floodgates opened.

Oh, Frank, Frank, Frank. What a ham for the camera, which sure wasn't me, although there was the time I covered a local *Peter Pan* production and strapped on a harness for my on-camera standup. *Oh, this is gonna be good*, I thought. But when the stagehand yanked the wire and launched me to the rafters, pain whooshed from below my belt and I barely squeezed out my lines, my voice so high it sounded like I'd sucked on a helium balloon. I learned my lesson the hard way: No more acting for the camera—it took a week before I could walk straight.

Frank had his way of reporting a story, and I had mine—I wondered if it took him a week to get his taste buds back. But, hey, different strokes for different folks. That's what makes life interesting. And I was about to visit an interesting place, one with all kinds of different flavors.

⎯⎯⎯⎯⎯⎯

We pulled into Sunni Sky's Homemade Ice Cream, and I told myself, *By all means, no sampling the spicy stuff and goofing around on camera.* I was a reporter, not an actor—*but it sure would be great if I could get somebody else to do that.*

I wasn't worried either about doing a story Frank had already done. Poor guy. He'd tortured himself on TV, but the station he worked for barely had any viewers. The Internet post had probably attracted some attention, but I figured the people who'd seen it wouldn't mind watching another version. They'd have ninety reasons to tune in.

"Ninety flavors?" I asked the long row of people seated in rocking chairs on Sunni Sky's front porch. They nodded up and down and bobbed back and forth. The ice-cream store resembled a ranch-style house, white with blue shutters and a picket fence. Folks lounged out front and licked and rocked, and I went down the line, interviewing one after another.

"Amazing."

"So many flavors."

"We love coming here."

"I think it's wonderful."

"Crumb cake," said a ginger-haired woman who planted her feet and pointed her cone at me. "Large pieces of crumb topping in there. See 'em? It's really good. Cinnamony and delicious."

I noticed a white board propped against the rail post with ice-cream flavors written in green marker. Some of them read like cocktail specials: Strawberry Daiquiri. White Russian. Piña Colada.

I thanked the row of rockers who nodded and bobbed without missing a lick. "Get yourself some crumb cake," the ginger-haired woman called as I opened the door to Sunni Sky's.

It was bright inside with lots of aluminum and glass and a few small tables. A giant blackboard covered one wall with more flavors listed top to bottom: Black Licorice. Egg Nogg. Rum Raisin. Pink Grapefruit. Tiramisu. Cake Batter.

Do people really eat this stuff? I wondered. Apparently they did. Sunni Sky's had a good crowd for a weekday afternoon in September.

"Ninety flavors, one hundred percent home-made," said Scott Wilson, store owner and mastermind. "How about some key lime pie ice cream?" he said, and when I didn't react, he suggested apple pie. "Getting ready to mix some now." I declined the apple, too, but told him some mixing video would be great.

"It really does taste like apple pie," he said while working his arms around the inside of a big metal bowl, though he admitted strawberry cheesecake was his favorite. Too bad he wasn't working up one of the daiquiris, I thought. Now if he had offered me one of those . . .

ORANGE CHOCOLATE. BROWNIE BATTER. SUGAR COOKIE. SO MANY CHOICES. PINEAPPLE. SOUR APPLE SHERBET. BLACK WALNUT. DIFFERENT STROKES FOR DIFFERENT FOLKS, BUT LIFE IS LIKE THAT. WE ALL HAVE TO FIND OUR OWN FLAVOR, BE IT COFFEE OR COLD SWEAT OR, GOODNESS KNOWS, EXIT WOUND.

Scott Wilson did not look like a typical ice-cream store owner. I tend to picture a skinny man in a white apron and paper hat, shaped like a triangle. Wilson was a tall, solid, football-tight-end type. "I think most people laughed when we said we were gonna start an ice-cream shop," he said.

He'd worked in the restaurant business up north. "You know, waiting tables, bartending. But we wanted our own little mom-and-pop shop, and that's really

how this started." He studied his large tight-end hands. "It also came down to prayer."

Had he been looking, he would have seen my mouth pop open, not that I was suddenly craving key lime. No, it was the part about prayer that surprised me. He wasn't a man full of just gummy worms and crumb cake. There was some real substance to Scott Wilson.

He told me he'd taken a leap of faith, thrown a Hail Mary of sorts. "The American dream," he said while mixing the apple pie, a dream that had led him to Angier of all places. He opened Sunni Sky's in 2003, and word spread, along with the flavors. Sugar cookie. Dirt cake. Dump cake. Rice Krispy Treat. People from two and three counties over came to marvel at the ice-cream concoctions. The names alone drew curiosity seekers—even the name of the store.

"My daughter's name is Sunni," Scott said, "spelled with an *i*. And my son is Skylar. We put the two together, and that's why it's called Sunni Sky's."

I decided right then Scott Wilson was a marketing genius. *But black licorice? Really?* I doubted that one had many takers. But what did it matter? National newspapers had written about all the creative flavors. *Good Morning America* once taped a spot at Sunni Sky's. Frank the ham had followed their lead, and now I had followed Frank's.

I asked Scott about the waiver form and Cold Sweat. "And what's that other flavor next to it?" I said, pointing to the board. "Exit Wound?"

"Oh, we've gotten a lot of attention for those."

No kidding, I thought.

He told me they included extra spicy sauces and habaneros and pointed to the form's bold print: **Hottest Known Peppers! Dangerously Hot!!** Cold Sweat was potent enough, but Exit Wound was even worse he said, and you weren't allowed to try Exit without first surviving Cold.

"Want some?" he asked, looking me square in the eyes, and there it was: the throwdown, the challenge, go all in, be a man, be aggressive, be the story—be Frank. *Or maybe somebody else can be Frank*, I mused.

"Maybe later," I said and stole a look around.

Nobody had signed away their pride while I'd been there, and none of the customers looked the least bit promising. I did notice a towheaded boy peering through the glass at the clay-colored ice cream but knew he wasn't about to get close to a habanero. No way, José. Youngsters weren't allowed near the spicy stuff.

The next best thing was a couple I interviewed who told me they'd once tried Cold Sweat. "Terrible, terrible," they garbled while shoveling scoops of huckleberry between their teeth—whatever huckleberry was. "We like spicy food, but Cold Sweat was nasty," they said—or I think that's what they said. I think they needed to pack their mouths with cold at the mere mention of Cold Sweat.

I turned to the big board again and studied the myriad of flavors. A ponytailed girl with dimples smiled at me from behind the counter, waiting to take my order. "Cold Sweat?" she said, all perky and cute and oblivious to my inner torment. Oh, the slings and arrows of outrageous fortune. To be or not to be Frank. Or Peter Pan. *Ughhh!*

"No," I finally muttered. "Think I'll just try some coffee ice cream. Single scoop, please, in a cake cone." I expected a disappointed frown, but what I got was that cute smile and dimples.

The agonizing decisions a reporter must make. How best to tell the story? Had I captured the essence of Sunni Sky's? I turned it over in my head as I stepped onto the porch and down the steps, cone in hand.

"Crumb cake? Did you get yourself some crumb cake?" the ginger-haired woman called to me. "Hope so. Crumb cake sure is good. Did you get some crumb cake?" I looked back to see her empty handed and leaning forward. I suspect she wanted another crumb cake cone for herself.

"Next time," I told her, and she laughed and kicked her feet, which sent the rocker rocking again.

"Attaboy!" she hooted.

I smiled and licked, the ice cream smooth and delicious, and felt perfectly content. I love coffee ice cream, but I did wonder about the crumb cake. And Cold Sweat. I thought of Frank and laughed, remembering his fire-engine face. "Water, water!" No doubt about it, he'd definitely captured the essence of that spicy specialty.

And I think I'd captured the essence of Sunni Sky's, maybe not like Frank had, but to each his own. Orange chocolate. Brownie batter. Sugar cookie. So many choices. Pineapple. Sour apple sherbet. Black walnut. Different strokes for different folks, but life is like that. We all have to find our own flavor, be it coffee or Cold Sweat or, goodness knows, Exit Wound.

"Ughhh!"

With ninety flavors Sunni Sky's had something for everyone, reporters included.

DOLLY'S DAIRY BAR

I WAS AT THE HOCKEY RINK IN RALEIGH WATCHING MY SON PLAY when one of the other peewee-hockey dads nudged me during a break in the action. He told me he watched the *Tar Heel Traveler* all the time. "Where you headin' next?" he asked. When I said Brevard, his face lit up like he'd just ripped a winning slap shot between the pipes. "You gotta go to Dolly's Dairy Bar," he exclaimed. "It's an ice-cream shop right there by the Pisgah National Forest. Best ice cream you ever had."

I was intrigued, but the ref had just dropped the puck and play had started again. I peered past the black scruff marks on the glass and cheered on number eleven. "Go, Scout, go!"

The dad watched, too. "Defense needs to step up," he muttered. "Look at that guy, he's wide open." His voice rose. "Get him!" he shouted, and after a moment, "You gotta get one. Best around. Delicious." I realized he wasn't talking about the defense anymore. "Some of the ice cream's named after summer camps, and they got a ton—camps *and* flavors."

I was about to ask him more, but Scout went rushing up the ice and fired a quick wrister that sailed past the goalie's glove and into the back of the net. "Yes!" I shouted and banged on the glass. "Attaboy!" Scout had just put his team ahead. And I had a feeling I might have scored, too.

I had been to Brevard before. The little town near Asheville is known for white squirrels, white from face to foot—their heads often have a trace of gray and their bodies a touch of brown if they've been rolling in mud. White squirrels are the size of gray squirrels but the color of polar bears and evoke warm and fuzzy feelings. They're part of Brevard's charm.

The story goes that in 1949 a carnival truck overturned in Florida, and two white squirrels on board escaped to a nearby pecan grove. The grove owner noticed them playing and was awed by their unusual color. He pointed them out to another man, and that man gave them to his niece in Brevard to keep as pets. But once in Brevard, one of them escaped again, and the remaining squirrel was apparently so heartbroken that it was set free to find its mate. Apparently, the "Adam and Eve squirrels" found each other—and their offspring found each other, too. Today thousands of white squirrels are believed to roam Transylvania County.

Many tend to congregate on the Brevard College campus, which I suppose make them smart squirrels. They certainly outfoxed us when we tried videotaping them. The darn critters hid from the camera, and the photographer and I spent an hour craning our necks and studying treetops. Two of them finally appeared, and we trained the lens on them every which way, captured them jumping, climbing, eating, resting. When we edited the piece later you would have thought we'd videotaped a whole storm of snowy squirrels. Lucky for us, white is white, and one looks like the other.

But to me Brevard comes in *two* colors: white and silver. It's home to the only museum in the world dedicated to vintage aluminum Christmas trees. Robert and I jumped in the car one December day and drove four hours just to shoot that single story. We walked into the Transylvania Heritage Museum where polished metal trees filled two large rooms, trees shinier than the silverware Nina and I use for special dinner guests, and each decorated in a particular theme. The Marilyn Monroe tree, for example, included photos of Marilyn dangling from the aluminum branches. She blew a pink bubblegum bubble in one picture, headlined BEING NORMAL IS BORING.

I interviewed Stephen Jackson, who began collecting the trees when a friend gave him a mangled one pulled from the trash—nice friend. Then somebody else picked one up for him at a yard sale. Twenty years later, Stephen had collected ninety aluminum trees and attracted widespread publicity. He'd been featured in the *New York Times* and on National Public Radio—and on WRAL. "Some of them are from 1959, so they're over fifty years old," he told me. He stood as tall as the tallest tree and looked almost as glittery in a gold retro sport coat he'd worn for the interview.

Now it was late August, and Robert and I were headed back to the Brevard area again to shoot more stories, including one on Dolly's Dairy Bar and the ice-cream flavors named after summer camps. I'd learned there were possibly more summer camps in Transylvania County than anywhere else in the country. I just hoped we hadn't already missed the campers; the start of school was only a week away.

Brevard is easy to find, and Dolly's should have been, too. The hockey dad had told me it was right by the forest entrance. "Can't miss it," he said—although he might have been talking about the defenseman who whiffed on a shot. But Robert and I somehow skipped the turn and arrived much later than planned.

It was a sunny afternoon, and to my delight there was a crowd. I sensed a good vibe. The place had a fun rustic look, a flat peachy-colored building with a long wooden porch and wide wooden chairs that leaned way back and snuggled the sitters who lounged beneath a row of soft yellow lightbulbs and ceiling fans. They ate and admired the scenery—distant mountains, lush greenery, and occasionally mountain bikers just coming off a forest trail and pedaling for home.

It was late in the day, much too late for a news crew cramming as many stories into an overnight road trip as possible. Our crazy detour had cost us precious time. We were due to meet a lady who cared for injured white squirrels—I couldn't get enough of those funny little critters—which gave us all of fifteen minutes to do what we could do at Dolly's. We'd have to come back the next day, although I'd already scheduled a sizable part of it to shoot some cyclists who were going to show us the twisty trails of the Pisgah National Forest—with a GoPro camera attached to one of the biker's helmets, I hoped.

"They come in, they come out," said the owner of Dolly's Dairy Bar, a man named Lee who'd only recently taken over and didn't plan to change a thing. His eyes traveled the shady road in front of the shop that disappeared behind the trees; the forest entrance was just around the bend. "They see ice cream after a long day's hike, and what better way to end it than with ice cream."

There were some ice-cream tongue twisters in the bunch: Kahdalea Avalanche, Chosatonga Cyclone, Illahee Swirl, Tekoa Brownie Fixation. I wondered if the campers could pronounce the names of their own camps.

Kids lounged in the chairs or sat on the porch rail, twirled around the porch post, or huddled about the picnic tables set beneath huge leafy trees at the edge

THE PLACE HAD A FUN RUSTIC LOOK, A FLAT PEACHY-COLORED BUILDING WITH A LONG WOODEN PORCH AND WIDE WOODEN CHAIRS THAT LEANED WAY BACK AND SNUGGLED THE SITTERS WHO LOUNGED BENEATH A ROW OF SOFT YELLOW LIGHTBULBS AND CEILING FANS.

of the parking lot. *Wow*, I thought, *all these kids. Now if we could only find as many white squirrels. The white squirrels . . .!* I checked my watch. *Oh, no.*

"We'll come back tomorrow," Robert said, packing the camera in the trunk. "The lady's waiting for us. Gotta go."

But I didn't want to go, not even for the sake of another white squirrel story, because a story can change, and moments tend to slip away—here today, gone tomorrow, like metal Christmas trees that lose their shine or end up in the trash. But Robert didn't seem so pessimistic. "We'll have time tomorrow, no problem. We'll make time. They'll be back," he said, pointing to the crowd. "People always eat ice cream."

"Yeah, I guess so," I said, not quite ready to close my notepad. I studied the ice cream flavors I'd copied from the board: Keystone Sunrise, Falling Creek Fantasy.

I told myself, *Well, maybe it will be okay tomorrow. Maybe the campers will still be around.* But I couldn't help feeling like a kid who'd taken the first lick of his scoop and accidentally rolled it off the cone and—*splat.* I looked again at the list, and staring back at me was Eagles Nest Meltdown. I felt I was having a meltdown of my own of sorts—or my story was.

North Carolina mountains are known for their pretty scenery—and changing weather. The next day was cloudy and fifteen degrees cooler. Not good for eating ice cream, but ideal for mountain biking. The morning shoot went great, especially the crazy GoPro shots. The bikes bumped and twisted through the forest, sometimes at frightening downhill speeds, cyclists bucked by rocks and tree roots but whooping as they raced pell-mell through the Pisgah.

We were exhilarated on the short drive to Dolly's, until we pulled into the empty parking lot. The porch was empty, too, not a single summer camper in sight, not even a Joe Shmoe nibbling on a single-scoop vanilla.

Robert busied himself with exterior shots. The peachy color showed up well, and I noticed cutesy road signs posted on a front beam: ICE CREAM AVE, SUNDAE STREET, BANANA SPLIT BOULEVARD. Robert also captured those.

A minivan finally rolled up, and a mom and her son hopped out; at least, I figured it was her son. He had a boyish face but towered over Mom—and me, too, for that matter.

He told me in a voice deeper than mine that he was a camp counselor. *This kid oughta be playing hockey*, I thought. *Bet he'd make a heck of a defenseman.* "Heading home," he said, "and wanted to stop at Dolly's on the way out of town." He took big bites of his mint chocolate chip, and the interview was over. And summer-camp season was, too. My only hope was for a few sentimental stragglers—one last Pinnacle Mountain Sensation or Green River Plunge before the journey back to school.

Late morning gave way to early afternoon and people did start to trickle in, like rays of sun on a Carolina Iceberg Blast. "The name of my camp is Gwynn Valley," said a boy about Scout's age. There was no doubt what ice cream he was ordering. "Gwynn Valley Gold Rush!" he exclaimed, with eyes as big as scoops. "Creamy caramel," he said and clutched it with both hands as though it was real gold, precious and rare.

I turned and did a double take at two blonde little girls who'd stepped up on the porch. They looked exactly alike from head to toe, and their grandmother told me, yep, they were identical twins. Grandma ordered for them, and we watched the girls eat their ice cream. "Love to see them smile," Grandma said, and I thought, *You can say that again. And again.*

The sun rose higher, and so did the temperature, and Dolly's quickly turned into a Highlander Explosion of sound bites:

"Delicious!"

"Ranks right up there with the best."

"I came here for the amazing scenery, but I didn't realize how amazing the ice cream would be."

I met Mary Childers, otherwise known as Dolly, whose bubbly personality and dark head full of bouncy curls seemed to fit her playful name. But Dolly admitted she was getting up in years, and so she'd sold the place but still stopped in almost every day. The camp flavors had been her idea long ago. "I love the kids," she said. "It's all about the kids. They support us, so we wanted to do something for them."

Dolly's offered more than fifty flavors, about half of them named for summer camps: Rockbrook Chocolate Illusion, Greenville Caveman Krunch, Lutheridge Lightning, Music Camp Obsession . . . the list went on.

The interview of the day went to an older couple seated close together on a bench under a tree, each of them enjoying an ice cream cone. I wondered if they were coming to pick up their grandkids from camp. But no, the man said. "This is our honeymoon," and his wife laughed and leaned against him. *Honeymoon?* I thought. "Fifty-seventh anniversary of a honeymoon!" he said and leaned against *her*.

What a picture they made, side by side, grinning like kids themselves. I should have asked what kind of ice cream they were eating but chose instead to imagine something cute and romantic. I glanced at my list and one name jumped out: Merrie-Woode Boo-Woop.

Robert and I lingered longer than usual. We watched the last of the campers and counselors pile into cars and pull away. A New Jersey family at the end of their vacation loaded up on sundaes and shakes and stood eating on the porch and told me it was the best ice cream they'd ever had.

I tried some myself and it *was* good, and the atmosphere added the perfect topping. This was a happy place. People associated Dolly's with kids and camps and summer fun and perhaps the best days of their lives. *Places like this are hard to find*, I thought.

I also began to think not just of ice cream but of rare white squirrels and vintage aluminum Christmas trees and magnificent mountain-biking trails. And I thought about summer and how I didn't want it to end.

The sun had ducked behind the clouds, and the front porch was empty again. Robert and I were looking at a long trip home. He stowed the gear and I opened the car door to climb in, but just before closing my notepad I took one last look at my list—and smiled at Pisgah Perfection.

Pro hockey was put on ice.

The NHL season should have been well underway in November 2012, but team owners and players were fighting over a contract, and it looked like the whole season might be a wash.

I love hockey, play hockey, and watch hockey. No hockey? I'm not sure who was more dejected, me or my son, Scout, who plays and watches, too. For a kid who doesn't like hot dogs, he was begging to visit Cloos' Coney Island. Cloos' is known for hot dogs. And hockey.

Scout needed his hockey fix, even if it was just gazing at players on a wall: a picture of Rod Brind'Amour, for example, clutching the Stanley Cup over his head, hair matted with sweat, eyes squeezed shut, mouth frozen in an agonizing victory cry.

I'd seen the video of that moment from June 19, 2006. The Carolina Hurricanes, that lowly underdog team from the South, had managed to win it all at home in a dramatic game seven. Most people in the crowd never even sat down. They stood and cheered during the whole game, and many had cried after the game out of elation and exhaustion.

Then came the trophy presentation, the hockey commissioner, stiff and formal in suit and tie on a strip of red carpet at center ice with microphone in hand, calling team captain Rod Brind'Amour to come stand beside him and then ignoring Brind'Amour while he delivered a few flowery remarks about the game and sport. Brind'Amour didn't wait for the commissioner to finish. He snatched the silver bowl, clutched both ends in a white-knuckled grip, hoisted it high, threw back his head, and screamed. He screamed like an uncaged animal freed at last, a jagged cry bottled far too long, packed full of pain and sacrifice and finally triumph. Brind'Amour screamed and stamped his feet on the red carpet as if trying to pound his skates through the fabric into the thick sheet below, to permanently imbed his blades into the ice.

Scout and I studied that frozen image on the wall at Cloos', which Dan Cloos had clipped from the newspaper the day after the game. He'd framed it, and by doing so seemed to sanctify it. His customers could witness Brind'Amour in his own private moment all over again, pouring out years of pent-up emotions. And if his silent scream didn't grab them, the headline shouting above him might: IT'S OURS!

"What a picture," I murmured, and Scout nodded without peeling his eyes from the Plexiglas.

My family and I ate at Cloos' once every couple of months but more than that during the NHL lockout. Dan was a Red Wings fan from Detroit and had scattered some of the team's memorabilia around the restaurant. Fortunately, he was a Hurricanes fan, too, and during those long empty weeks without hockey we could at least sit and eat and surround ourselves with hockey. There were plenty of other sports on the walls, too, including anything NC State, and of course, all things Detroit. A Tigers' ballplayer leaped from the pitching mound and pumped his fists behind another pane. The headline above him read GR-RR-RR-EAT!

"You really should do a story," Nina said for the tenth time. "So what if Cloos' is behind the station."

Convenient interview, I thought, remembering that old news director. I could practically hear him spitting the words. *A story on a restaurant behind the TV station? Lazy!* I saw him again shaking his head and clucking his tongue. *Tsk, tsk.* The man still haunted me.

Dan threw us a wave and a smile from the grill. "Mr. Tar Heel Traveler!" he announced. "Where you going this week?" He wore a blue T-shirt that read WORLD SERIES CHAMPIONS.

"Staying close to home," I called across the countertop. He laughed and went back to the chopping block. He sold a lot of Philly cheesesteaks.

I'd been on the road lately and had replenished the story stockpile, and I needed to stay at the station and write for a few days. But it's near torture to let a whole week slip by without shooting, sort of like pulling the drain from a watery hole in the desert. I fear being left high and dry. *If only we could shoot at least one story* . . .

My eyes skipped across the sports page I'd tucked under my arm when I walked from the station to meet Nina and Scout, and I flopped it open while waiting for my cheeseburger with extra mayo. The hockey lockout was spread across the front page. Raleigh had become a hockey hotbed of sorts, and I was happy the local paper devoted so much ink to it. I skimmed the first few lines, but it was noisy in Cloos', and I looked up and took in the happy commotion, and my eyes once again drifted to the silent scream. And there in that moment I felt something shift—or rather, lift. There was a reason to do a story now on Cloos'. Hockey was on ice and questions lingered, and each passing day of the lockout drained hopes of saving the season, and if it could be saved, would fans even return?

But at Cloos' I felt the passion was still there, between those memorabilia-decked walls. People loved this place, embraced it with a kind of white-knuckled grip, and in my own private moment Brind'Amour's silent scream drowned out everything else. He hoisted the Stanley Cup, and I squelched the voice of my old news director and his haunting refrain.

No, this would not be just a convenient interview. It would be a story about hockey and passion and people who clung to a special place called Cloos'—and believed, "IT'S OURS!"

I'll mention only the highlights for fear of being anticlimactic because, after all, I'd already overcome my adversary, that grouchy old news director, and just doing the story amounted to victory. But still, I told no one in the newsroom where we were off to. They probably thought just another Tar Heel Traveler trip when they saw Robert and me shove out the door. The trip took us two minutes to travel.

You can always guarantee a lunchtime crowd at Cloos', and that November day did not disappoint. I walked in and looked down the length of that long aisle, and I had to smile. *Perfect.* Seats occupied, people laughing, waitresses scurrying, Dan chopping, and nobody paying our camera much attention, even when Robert started firing away. That's what I like about Cloos'. Folks act natural, nothing fancy, nothing forced, and nothing to get in the way of their favorite mealtime get-away. They're going to enjoy themselves; they can't help themselves. It's the place, the atmosphere. Cloos' is a bright space with white walls and a checkerboard floor and splashes of NC State red and Detroit Lions blue, Detroit Tigers black, and Michigan Wolverines yellow, and red again for those hockey Hurricanes. And ESPN plays on an overhead TV.

"I don't think I've ever been in a place that's more comfortable," said a man leaning against the counter. My first sound bite of the day set the tone.

Except on this day Dan was not so comfortable. I sensed it even before he spilled the beans. He kept mashing the same burger till it was flat as a slice of cheese, and when he draped it with a slice of cheese he mistakenly mashed it again.

He admitted he was nervous in front of a camera but also humbled. He'd faithfully watched my travels on TV. "And now you're here," he said and spread his arms, one hand still holding the goopy spatula. "I can't believe it. I'm honored."

He told me about moving from Michigan and opening Cloos' in 1988, and after twenty-five years he now felt more like a North Carolinian than a Michigander. But he still had links to home. His hot dogs came from Detroit. "And I drive to the airport myself and pick them up." Viva La Detroit! screamed a sign on the counter.

Dan didn't seem nervous anymore and chatted away. "You'd be amazed at the number of people who come in here because of our ice."

"Ice?"

"Some people come here just to get the ice." Dan had a cooler full of crushed ice, and Robert captured a waitress plunging a scooper all the way to the handle and lifting a glistening mound. The video was good, but the sound was great: crushed ice crushing into a plastic cup. I made a note in my pad: *ice*. And next to it I wrote *Brind'Amour*.

People talked about the great french fries, the hot dogs and hamburgers, chicken pitas, and Philly cheesesteaks. They told me how long they'd been coming to Cloos'. Twenty-three years, said an NC State grad who'd discovered it during school and was still a regular.

"The chaos is awesome," said a cute cashier who was finishing up at NC State. "I like when it's busy. It keeps us going."

I made my way to the back, to the table with the little paper sign that read, Reserved for Cloos' Club, and sure enough there was Sandy, who I knew from church and who I saw every time I came to Cloos'. She threw her arms open when I walked up as if saying, *Hooray* or *Touchdown*. Then again, maybe not.

"The girls always complain that the guys here, all they talk about is sports. But there's more girl talk than sports talk at our table." Her three friends nodded and giggled. "I mean, this is our therapy."

"Well, what *do* you talk about?" I asked.

"We talk about everything." Her eyes twinkled. "Everything."

"We get more news per calorie than anywhere else you could go," chimed another Cloos' Club regular who began describing the Coney Islands in detail. "They pop," she said. "They have a crunchy outside casing, and they pop when you bite them."

The ladies kept breaking off the interview to greet people they recognized. "Hey, Julie. Hey, girl!" They wrapped Julie in a big group hug. "How are youuuu? Look, we're on TVEEEE!" and they pointed at the camera and laughed hysterically.

The Cloos' Club could have been a story all by itself. The ladies had been eating lunch together for almost twenty years. "I'm a Friday only," one of them said. "But she's every day," pointing to Sandy, who smiled with a sheepish grin. They also pointed to the little picture that hung above their heads. It showed about ten women crowding around and smiling for the camera. The Cloos' Club had earned a place on the wall.

It was the wall that attracted me, all the colorful sports memorabilia. I took note of the street signs that hung cockeyed just below the ceiling: RED WINGS DR., DETROIT TIGERS AVE., WOLFPACK AVE., CLOOS' RD. I made sure Robert also shot the one that said, HOCKEYTOWN. "And shoot Brind'Amour," I said, apparently not for the first time, and Robert sighed and lugged the camera onto his shoulder. I guess he'd shot it half a dozen times already. We probably had more minutes of that photo than Brind'Amour had career goals, but I couldn't help myself. To me, the picture was the story.

"These people are like my family," said the cute cashier.

"We just love what we do," said Dan. "We're all very lucky." He spread his arms again and gave the camera a wide cheesy grin. "And the owner is so good looking!"

He probably didn't think I'd use that last bit of sound in my story, but I was pretty sure I would because it seemed to capture his personality, and, besides, it was a good way to end the piece. I turned to my pad.

Smile, Dan, I wrote. *You've found a home. And . . . IT'S OURS!*

SACRED PLACES
(THE FINAL CUP)

THERE ARE SACRED PLACES IN MY LIFE, PLACES THAT ARE DEEPLY special to me, and when I set foot on their grounds, I grow instantly quiet, as if their beauty and meaning are almost too much to absorb.

One of them is my alma mater. When I return to Washington and Lee I actually get chills. The rolling front lawn is manicured and beautiful, and I try hard to take it all in. My eyes pan the lush grass and rise slowly up the slope to the top, inevitably to the top, to the enormous white columns towering above, a perfect row of them, round and gleaming in the sun. They're like proud sentinels protecting the stately brick buildings behind them, a neat row of them, too, and when the sun strikes the bricks, they appear as red as the stripe on an American flag.

I'm almost afraid to step from the walkway, the grass is so pristine, but it's more than that. I'm keenly aware of those who have tread before me, and my eyes pan down the slope, sweep across the wide swath of lawn to the bottom, inevitably to the bottom, to the stone chapel opposite the colonnade. Inside rests the body of Robert E. Lee.

Lee traveled to the Shenandoah Valley of Virginia after the Civil War to become president of the university that now bears his name. And George Washington's name, too. Washington saved the school from financial ruin almost a century before.

Washington and Lee. Lee's body lies in a chapel crypt, and opposite the chapel a statue of Washington poses atop the highest brick building. I feel a great sense of honor and tradition, duty and country, and it's no wonder I'm antsy about setting my loafer on the grass. And yet in a far corner of the lawn barefoot kids in gym shorts and T-shirts are tossing a Frisbee, and I think, *Yes, it's good to be back*, and I do take that step. I walk the lawn between Washington and Lee, feeling chills but also pride and love for this sacred place.

Route 128 ends at the roundabout in Gloucester. I take the third exit, drive a few miles and turn left at the white church where the road dips and narrows. Most people don't know to take that left; there's no sign pointing to Annisquam.

I spent every summer of my life in this little village on the North Shore of Massachusetts, and it's not chills I get when the road curves past the old stone chair and weathered Cape Cods but a deep sense of place, isolated and distinct. How fortunate I feel to be part of it, and it is a permanent part of me no matter how far I roam.

The road empties at the Village Hall, and I bear left, then right at the old footbridge and drive slowly alongside the Annisquam River, admiring the harbor, the gently bobbing boats, and water winking in the sun.

My friends call Annisquam the bubble, protected and safe and everything within walking distance. The memories are never far out of reach, either: diving off the Old Wharf Lot dock, swimming at Cambridge Beach, climbing Squam Rock, tennis matches and sailboat races and sunsets over Ipswich Bay. The same families have lived here for generations.

I stop at Nick's house on River Road, lean out the window and holler, "Yeah, buddy!" and a moment later Nick and my other buddy Jamie come bounding out, laughing and pumping my hand and hooting a "Yeah, buddy" of their own. It's another July, a year since I've been back, and we clamber inside and raid the fridge—Rolling Rocks all around. We wind through the kitchen and step onto the porch, and for just an instant the laughter dies and nobody says a word or tips their bottle back. Because it's the view we drink in: the water and boats and beach across the way, the majesty and serenity of what we see. And again it's almost too much to take in, like gazing at a masterpiece, mesmerized by the beauty but always an arm's length away. Sometimes I wonder if I'm in the bubble or outside it. But what I do know is I'm part of it, part of Annisquam, and it's part of me. And I am home.

My finger slips off the key, and I consider the word I've just typed: "*home.*" I fumble for my mug, swish my coffee, "home" circling my head. It's a few minutes and a sip or two before I click the computer key Up arrow, scroll back, and read the last two pages I've written. Too flowery maybe? Well, but it's the end of the book and I'm trying to make a point, and I suppose the point is "Home." Period.

Washington and Lee and Annisquam are places where I belong. *"Sacred"*? Too strong a word? I swish my coffee again and consider the title I've given my last chapter and raise the mug to my lips without taking my eyes from the screen. But then I do look away because the coffee's tasty, and I wonder just how many cups I've had. Too many probably, but at least I switched to decaf. Matter of fact, here she comes again with the orange-handled pot. She always knows when I'm on my last sip. Never fails.

"Almost done," I tell her, guilty for hogging the table. "Promise."

She tilts the pot. "No worries, honey. Take your time, shug. Get you anything else?"

Words, I want to tell her. Can you give me the right words? I think she hears me thinking. She studies me with a hand on her hip and smiles very sweetly before turning away, and even after she does the smile stays with me.

"Home." The word glows on the screen, and I think if home is where I feel I belong, a place of comfort and security and part of my identity, then *this* is home, the diner on the corner where I sit at my usual table by the window and drink gobs of coffee and write about drinking gobs of coffee. This is who I am, the guy in the zone tapping his thoughts on a laptop, a creature of habit who frequents the same place, sits at the same table, eats the same breakfast every morning—two scrambled, toast, grits, and coffee. Well, occasionally bacon if I feel adventurous. I love it. And the food's pretty good, too.

What I love is sitting here with my breakfast and my thoughts. What absolute peace it is. Gosh, I'm happy at my little table, so utterly content. And I'm sure I'm not the only one.

I have visited so many great little restaurants on my Tar Heel travels, sat at countless counters enjoying bacon and eggs, hot dogs and hamburgers, barbecue and biscuits and donuts and ice cream. "Who's got the best?" people always want to know. "Best barbecue?" they ask. "How 'bout the hot dogs? Whaddya think? Where should I go for ice cream?" I usually dodge the questions. Truth is, I hate to play favorites because I feel loyal to them all and don't want to betray any place. I feel a kind of kinship with these landmarks, which is really what they are. And I hope they don't fall by the wayside.

But I don't think they will. Because I sense there are people like me who get up every day, walk out the door of their home and through the door of their

WHAT I LOVE IS SITTING HERE WITH MY BREAKFAST AND MY THOUGHTS. WHAT ABSOLUTE PEACE IT IS. GOSH, I'M HAPPY AT MY LITTLE TABLE, SO UTTERLY CONTENT. AND I'M SURE I'M NOT THE ONLY ONE.

other "home," where they visit with friends they love. And, oh yeah, eat a good meal. But it's not the food that comes first. It never was about the food.

I don't want it to end, "it" being these beloved hole-in-the-wall, mom-and-pop places I consider sacred; that is, if sacred means safe, secure, special, warm, cozy, comforting. I don't want it to end—the breakfast, the lunch, the hour or two or, goodness me, three I spend at my little table. But sooner or later you come to the final cup and settle the bill and thank the nice waitress and rise from your seat and step back into the world, leaving home behind. "Home." Yes, it feels like home.

"See you tomorrow, honey," she says and waves. "I'll have the coffee ready for you." She smiles, and, goodness gracious, so do I, a great big grin that stays with me even after I wave back and turn for the door, despite the tug at my heart wishing I could stay and spend another hour or two or maybe the whole day and never leave. But then, there *is* tomorrow and another order of eggs and another cup of coffee and another page or two to write. And another hour or two or three to spend at home.

Of course, my real home is the "sideways house," my own house, the only house in my neighborhood that sits sideways to the street. There's a hockey net in the driveway, and most days after school my son, Scout, ties on roller skates and shoots pucks, and sometimes I join him. My daughters are hockey players, too, though Lane is away at college now studying journalism, and Genie is interested in film and just started driving. They're good kids and parts of them are just like me, but they all look like Nina with brown hair and brown eyes.

Nina is a loving mom and wife, a great mom and wife, and I've dragged her to many greasy spoons over the years when she'd rather have been eating a salad at a restaurant with unchipped china and polished floors. But she appreciates southern hospitality, old-time traditions and memorable characters—and good pancakes. I talk to her about the book over my two scrambled with bacon, and she shakes her head. "When are you ever gonna finish the thing?"

"I know, I know," I say and gulp my coffee while the conversation shifts and Nina talks about something I'll soon forget. I live in a zone when I work on a book, and it can be hard to bust out when real life knocks.

So I thank Nina for putting up with me and for most times saying, "No, you go ahead. I'll get something to eat later," and off I'd slink to a breakfast dive alone, just me and my laptop, and type for a couple hours, morning after morning for weeks and months on end.

I'm a slow writer anyway, and as I began to delve into all the diners I'd visited I realized these weren't stories I could just dash off—or maybe I could, but I felt they deserved more. It struck me that each chapter was like its own little morality play. The restaurants taught lessons about working hard and earning an honest dollar, treating folks well and living right—though not necessarily about eating right.

It was tough finding the right words and crafting the manuscript, and who knows how many cups of coffee I downed or how high my cholesterol soared while I sat and ate and sipped and pecked. I read bits and pieces to Nina and to Lane, Genie, and Scout, especially when I was stuck or unsure about a word or phrase or even a whole chapter, and they all gave me positive feedback. They also said, "When are you ever gonna finish the thing?" Mom, Dad, my sister, and her family also read sections and offered sound advice—and repeated the refrain. "When are you ever . . . ?"

I ate up so many mornings working on the book I didn't have enough time to write Tar Heel Traveler stories during the day, so I'd finish those at home after dinner, often working late into the night. Except for the third Monday night of every month.

Those third Mondays I'd be at the Page-Walker house in Cary sitting in a third-floor room, bare except for the uneven table and eight other writers seated around it. We don't have an official name—I call it the Cary Writers' Club—but it's been around for about twenty years. I joined back when only one of us had been published. Now almost everybody at the lopsided table has a book out, and we spend time talking about editors and agents and even royalty checks. We also take turns critiquing each other's manuscripts, and I'm afraid I hogged the time over the past two dozen monthly Mondays and submitted more chapters than I should have. But my fellow writers never complained. It wasn't, "Oh, cripes, not another hot dog story!" but rather, "Let's critique Scott's. Who wants to start?" They were good sports about reading my litany of food stories, and their analysis was always thorough. That third floor is bare only in terms of furniture. Creativity and ideas are abundant.

At one of our Monday night meetings somebody mentioned the book *Olive Kitteridge* by Elizabeth Strout, and I picked it up the next day at the library. The book won the Pulitzer Prize, and the story pulled me in—and so did the back of the book that mentioned Strout's career. I was surprised to read she's on the faculty at Queens University of Charlotte and teaches in the MFA program on creative writing. I didn't know Queens offered a master's degree in creative writing and scrambled to my laptop to research it. I learned it was a low-residency program—spend two weeks a year on campus and do the rest of the work online. Before I knew it I was enrolled.

I started *Tar Heel Traveler Eats* at about the same time. I arrived at Queens for my first weeklong stay with two hot dog manuscripts under my arm and thought, *What in the world am I doing? I'm way over the hill and I'll be living in a dorm with hip, young, perky writers from all over the map at one of the country's top MFA writing programs, and I'm gonna show up to my critique session with stories about hot dogs. Holy moly.*

But to my surprise several other students had lines on their faces and gray in their hair. I enjoyed reading sections of their memoirs, how they survived illness, unemployment, abandonment, homelessness, beatings, kidnappings . . . *jeez.* And then there were the hot dogs.

I forced myself to pry the pages from under my arm and hand them out, wincing as I did. "This is something just a little different. . . ." I began, cringing as they started reading and wishing they'd waited to dig in back in their dorm rooms. But they kept reading and there wasn't a single guffaw. Nobody crumpled my papers and aimed a three-pointer for the trash can.

Instead, my instructors and fellow students at Queens gave me useful suggestions, often causing me, rightly, to rewrite entire chapters. And after many submissions and countless critiques over several semesters, they'd occasionally cock their heads and look at me and say, "When you ever gonna finish that thing?"

I teamed up with some fine photographers while visiting restaurants near and far. I worked with a rotating group when I first set out as the Tar Heel Traveler in September 2007, one photographer for six months and another for six months, and so on. Management didn't want them to shoot features too long for fear they'd forget how to tune in live shots and cover real news. But I think the station also took care to spread the fun around. Hard-news photographers would trudge back to the station having chased criminals around all day in the rain, sleet, or snow, and I'd walk through the door at the same time with a silly grin, a full belly, and complimentary box of donuts.

Robert Meikle jumped at the chance to wander the back roads and slip into diners. It's always good to work with someone from the same generation who appreciates the nostalgia of a good mom-and-pop. Robert's actually a year older than I am but, unlike me, has no gray hair; in fact, he doesn't have any hair at all. He's bald and wears glasses and leaves the nice waitresses big tips. Robert was behind the camera on a great many of my restaurant visits, and I think he enjoyed shooting and editing the stories as much as he did eating all the delicious homemade food. His creativity brought the restaurants to life and accented their down-to-earth values.

Robert eventually became the permanent Tar Heel Traveler photographer. After a few rotations, management scrapped the merry-go-round idea, realizing how difficult it was for somebody new to step into the role—the stories are fun but can be intensely complicated to put together, though Robert doesn't seem to mind the strain. As far as he's concerned, the more complicated the piece, the more creative he can be. I have a feeling Robert and I will be eating a lot more meals together in the Tar Heel Traveler years ahead.

Tom Normanly and Greg Clark also shot many of the food features I've written, and I can't thank them enough for their dedication and passion.

It was Greg who joined me at Hap's Grill in Salisbury and Dick's Hotdog Stand in Wilson, among others, but he was so hardworking and focused that I'm not sure he ever had the chance to eat. I must buy him lunch sometime, and dessert, too. And a jumbo cup of iced tea.

Tom spent two years as the Tar Heel Traveler photographer, and what a blast we had rambling around North Carolina. He loved meeting Hot Dog George at the Roast Grill in Raleigh and shooting all those airplanes at the

Pik N Pig in Carthage—although his hearing may never be the same. I owe him lunch, dessert, iced tea, and earplugs, plus a big thanks for being so jovial and fun loving on those and many other stories.

I thank Globe Pequot for publishing *Tar Heel Traveler Eats* and my first book, *Tar Heel Traveler: Journeys across North Carolina.* What a professional job the staff did on both. So what's next, you ask? Number three in the series? *Hmm.* Lemme think on it over coffee.

Both Tar Heel Traveler books use lots of pictures, which are actually freeze-frames plucked from my restaurant stories that aired on TV. That's why there are many good action shots of people chomping on hot dogs and cooks smothering burgers with cheese—we captured the action with our video camera. But how to convert video freeze frames to the printed page? It can get complicated, so I once again called on Kelly Gardner at WRAL.com who said no problem and converted them without a hitch. The photos add so much to the book, both books, and I thank him doubly for his great expertise.

I owe WRAL-TV much gratitude for allowing me to hang up my suits and ties and wear jeans and cowboy boots—yep, I do love playing the cowboy. I believe I have the best job in television, and I don't mean the best TV job in Raleigh or North Carolina but nationwide. There aren't many full-time feature reporters anymore, possibly fewer than five, and I'm so fortunate to be one of them, and not only that but to work in North Carolina, a wondrous state to explore, full of beauty and history and southern hospitality.

It's the old-timey restaurants that embody southern hospitality, which is why I find them so appealing, and not just appealing but important. Maybe there's not enough southern hospitality in the world. Perhaps we should preserve what we have.

I know there will be readers who get to this part of the book and say, "What?! This is the end? But you didn't write about___. You missed the story on___."

I know, I know. There are many, many restaurants I haven't visited yet that also deserve time on the page. They should be honored, too, and I've already started a list that continually grows. My belly growls every time I look at it, and my hand begins to ache. It's the pre-stages of writer's cramp. *Hmm.* I feel a sequel beginning to percolate like a fresh pot of coffee.

Time to hit the road again and keep my eyes peeled for a little place with a faded awning and an OPEN sign hanging crooked in the window and a rusty bell above the door that dings when you step inside and a wooden floor worn from seventy-five years of shuffling feet. I'll slip into a booth and order from the nice waitress and power up my laptop.

And I'll thank the good heavens for places such as this.

B's Barbecue
751 B's Barbeque Road
Greenville, NC 27858
No phone listed

Bessie
Dairy Queen
1837 Southeast Boulevard
Clinton, NC 28328
(910) 592-1844

Bill's Barbecue (aka Bill Ellis' Barbecue)
3007 Downing Street
Wilson, NC 27893
(252) 237-4372 or (800) 68-BILLS
bills-bbq.com

Bill's Hot Dogs
109 Gladden Street
Washington, NC 27889
(252) 946-3343
facebook.com/billshotdog

Britt's Donuts
11 Boardwalk
Carolina Beach, NC 28428
(910) 707-0755

Bud's Grill
1601 North Main Street
Tarboro, NC 27886
(252) 823-5665

Capt'n Franks Hot Dogs
800 North Croatan Highway
Kitty Hawk, NC 27949
(252) 261-9923
captnfranks.com/

Central Cafe
132 South Church Street
Rocky Mount, NC 27804
(252) 446-8568
facebook.com/pages/Central-Cafe/153459041361252

City Lunch Cafe
5 South Main Street
Franklinton, NC 27525
(919) 494-5815
facebook.com/pages/City-Lunch-CAFE-also-known-as-THE-HOT-DOG-Stand/235958746436223

Cloos'
2233 Avent Ferry Road, #102
Raleigh, NC 27606
(919) 834-3354

Clyde Cooper's Barbecue
327 South Wilmington Street
Raleigh NC 27601
(919) 832-7614
clydecoopersbbq.com/

Dick's Hotdog Stand
1500 Nash Street North
Wilson, NC 27893
(252) 243-6313
dickshotdogstand.com/

Dolly's Dairy Bar
128 Pisgah Highway
Pisgah Forest, NC 28768
(828) 862-6610
facebook.com/dollysicecream

Flo's Kitchen
1015 Goldsboro Street South
Wilson, NC 27893
(252) 237-9146

Hap's Grill
116½ North Main Street
Salisbury, NC 28144
(704) 633-5872
facebook.com/pages/Haps-Grill-INC/162923337079641

Jim's Ole Time Hot Dogs
2000 Walnut Street
Cary, NC 27518
No phone listed

Johnson's Hamburgers
1520 East 11th Street
Siler City, NC 27344
No phone listed
facebook.com/pages/Johnsons-Siler-City-NC/148435321834257

Jones Lunch
415 East Main Street
Clayton, NC 27520
(919) 553-7528

Merritt's Store & Grill
1009 South Columbia Street
Chapel Hill, NC 27514
(919) 942-4897
merrittsstoreandgrill.com/

Parker's Barbecue
2514 US Highway 301
Wilson, NC 27893
(252) 237-0972

Paul's Place
11725 US Highway 117
Rocky Point, NC 28457
(910) 675-2345
facebook.com/PaulsPlaceHotDogs

Pik N Pig
194 Gilliam McConnell Road
Carthage, NC 28327
(910) 947-7591
pik-n-pig.com

The Roast Grill
7 South West Street
Raleigh, NC 27603
(919) 832-8292
roastgrill.com

Sherry's Bakery
22 North Wilson Avenue
Dunn, NC 28334
(910) 892-3310
sherrysbakery.com

Shorty's Famous Hot Dogs
214 South White St.
Wake Forest, NC 27587
(919) 556-8026

Sunni Sky's Homemade Ice Cream
8617 NC Highway 55
Angier, NC 27501
(919) 427-7118
sunniskys.com

Walter's Grill
317 East Main Street
Murfreesboro, NC 27855
(252) 398-4006
facebook.com/waltersgrill?rf=115927891769034

Wilber's Barbecue
4172 US Highway 70 East
Goldsboro, NC
(919) 778-5218 or (919) 778-5219
wilbersbarbecue.com

Yum Yum Better Ice Cream
1219 Spring Garden Street
Greensboro, NC 27403
(336) 272-8284
facebook.com/yumyumbettericecreamandhotdogs

INDEX

ABOUT THE AUTHOR

Scott Mason has been a television reporter for over thirty years and for WRAL's *Tar Heel Traveler* since 2007. His more than one hundred journalism awards include twenty regional Emmys and three National Edward R. Murrow Awards. He has twice been named North Carolina Television Reporter of the Year, in 2004 and 2005. He is also the author of the book *Tar Heel Traveler: Journeys across North Carolina* (Globe Pequot).